COMMUNALISATION OF INDIAN SOCIETY

COMMUNALISATION OF INDIAN SOCIETY
A Sociological Analysis

Arvinder A. Ansari

COMMUNALISATION OF INDIAN SOCIETY
A Sociological Analysis
Arvinder A. Ansari

Published in 2012

Published by
AAKAR BOOKS
28 E Pocket IV, Mayur Vihar Phase I, Delhi 110 091
Phone : 011 2279 5505 Telefax : 011 2279 5641
info@aakarbooks.com; www.aakarbooks.com

Printed at
Arpit Printographers, Delhi 110 032
arpitprinto@yahoo.com

CONTENTS

FOREWORD

Communalism remains a subject of perennial concern and interest. It is hardly surprising that young scholars take it up for study and research. It is another matter if they are able to break new ground or come out with a refreshing perspective to understand its myriad dimensions.

Dr. Arvinder Ansari has been engaged in the study of communalism from the beginning of her academic career. She undertook a study of communalism, more particularly Hindu-Muslim tensions and conflict based on secondary sources. She moved on to a study of Hindu-Sikh conflict, focussing specifically on the Sikh riots during the early 1980s. She has used this background to now come up with a synoptic treatment and analysis of communalism.

Many years ago, I had argued that an almost exclusive focus on Hindu-Muslim conflict as if it was a unique kind of conflict, was detrimental to an understanding of communalism. There was need to place Hindu-Muslim communalism together with other forms of inter-community tensions and conflicts so that their similarities and differences as well as their distinct nature could be gauged. Dr. Ansari has recognised this broadened perspective, what she has to say does testify to this comparative orientation.

Dr. Ansari has chosen to focus in this study on the process of growing communalisation of society during the past several decades. Communalisation is a complex and many-layered phenomenon. It has to be worked through many levels. The first is the state and its interaction with the society. The state may be secular, committed to maintaining a wall of separation between state and religion. However, if the society is not sufficiently secularised, which continues to be the case in India, sooner or later the social processes built around communitarian identities and claims are likely to assert themselves and compromise the secular credentials of the state. One can easily contend that the state started out with strong secular pretensions, but the deep-seated communitarian ethos and orientations forced it to make numerous compromises. As a result, the very meaning of secularism was transformed. As the architect of modern India, Nehru and so many others within his party were committed to the meaning of secularism as having nothing to do with religion. However, Nehru could not adhere to this meaning and increasingly spoke of secularism as equal respect to all religions. Thus, the interaction between the state and society is one area that one is perforce required to deal with towards understanding the communalisation of the polity and society.

The second dimension that requires exploration is the nature of social change in India and how that change has impacted on the society and its culture. There is an old wisdom that holds that the illiterate and rural people are less drawn towards communalism even as they may firmly believe in and practise their religion. Communalism is a virus that afflicts the middle class and those who have registered social mobility. If this proposition is taken up seriously, then exploration of the communalisation of society must delve deeply into the sudden growth of a new middle class over the past two decades or more and the increased possibilities of social mobility where possibilities of such rapid social mobility were virtually absent. Emergence of the middle class and increased social mobility bring with them changes in lifestyle, which results in widespread wearing of religious symbols in the public sphere, elaborate celebration of religious rituals and festivals, such as Durga Puja, Id-e-milad-un-Nabi or birth anniversaries of gurus and saints. Where a community is not able to draw upon such mobilisation resources from its past cultural legacy, the effort is often to invent idols so that the community does not lag behind other communities. Further reinforcement of communitarian orientations is brought about by religious tourism so that those enthusiastic to demonstrate or flaunt their communitarian identity travel in hordes in chartered buses to unknown shrines which thereby shoot into prominence and come alive as a means of legitimating communitarian ethos and practices.

The third dimension is the rise of religious parties which use the growing communalisation to push their agenda of speaking in the name of a community and seeking to rework the polity so as to ensure that the community has a decisive dominance within the nation. Religious parties have been in existence from the time of the early rise of nationalism in India, but they never enjoyed a high degree of salience in public life. If anything, they were peripheral to the political system and its processes. However, since the late 1980s, which incidentally coincides with the rise of the new middle class and increased social mobility, religious parties have come to occupy a salience they never had. It is true that religious parties have not had remarkable electoral success and never emerged as the majority party at the national level. Nonetheless, the remarkable support they enjoyed at one time and continue to do within pockets of their communities is a phenomenon that cannot be adequately understood without reference to communalisation widely growing within the society.

The fourth dimension is education and educational processes. From the time of Independence, the state has reposed a great deal of trust in promoting modernisation and national integration. However, this trust was misplaced and misguided as using education for national integration threatened people's sense of belonging to their community and identity. Such an approach has over the years come under questioning from the democratic point of view. This has precipitated concern for an approach that encourages acceptance of diversity as a condition of life, allows communities free to work out their destinies while at the same time drawing limits to how far communitarian claims should be pressed. One would be off the mark if one were to suggest that a broad consensus over these issues has emerged, but it is indicative of the direction in which the county should move if it has to tide over communalisation. Until such consensus is articulated, education continues to feed into the process of communalisation of society as the pupils arrive with their cultural package and the teachers, who also come from roughly the same background with similar profiles, are not willing to challenge and dismantle established stereotypes and family values. This is a serious dilemma and its implications and consequences for communalisation of society deserve to be looked at seriously.

Dr. Ansari's study should act as a spur to others to take up the study of the communalisation issue and explore it more deeply. Focussing on macro processes in the study of communalism which was the order of the day at one time, particularly when the study of communalism first came to be made, but it is time that we now move on to micro processes which are crucial to understanding what makes people communal or communally inclined.

New Delhi
July 12, 2011

Imtiaz Ahmad

PREFACE

Communalism is a complex phenomenon. Many discussions have been taking place on this issue, more rigorously in the past two and a half centuries. Until recently, in common parlance it used to be argued that communalism is essentially a creation of British imperialism and after the withdrawal of the British from India communal tensions would disappear—that is how the folklore of Indian history used to be described. Yet, sixty-five years after Independence, we find that communal tensions have not disappeared, in fact, they have got aggravated.

Thus the society we have inherited from the colonial period was a communalised society and no conscious efforts were made in the post-Independence period to get rid of this communal legacy. On the one hand our society was communally divided and on the other, politicians reinforced this communal division for their electoral purposes.

The rising trend of communalism and the accompanying violence has created a feeling of insecurity among the religious minorities and ethnic groups. Muslims, in particular, fear discrimination and confrontation after the Gujarat 2002 riots. This may be plain fear but the nation cannot afford to let about one-sixth of the country's population fall victim to panic, suspicion and insecurity. The events between 1984 and 2002 in Punjab, Kashmir, Uttar Pradesh, Bihar, Assam, Delhi, Surat and Gujarat give ample evidence and a taste of the destructive outcome of the communal virus in its varied forms.

Communalism operates at different levels ranging from

individual relations and interests to the local institutional and national politics and to communal riots. There is a whole range of social relations and politics over which communalism pervades today and this spread of communalism involves two inter-related central issues. The first is the state of consciousness in society. The second is communalism as an instrument of power, not purely for capturing state power but for operating in political, social and economic domains and at almost all levels of social organisation.

Common identity based on religion is an integral factor in the existing state of social consciousness in our society. It provides an identity of being part of a community to all those who believe in the same religion. It is this belief in commonality which is used for communal mobilisation. The community identity based on religious consciousness is manipulated for purposes of power at various levels by certain political parties. This mobilisation of sections of society on the basis of religious belief for the purpose of power is central to the intensification of communalism today.

Communist ideology is an instrument of political parties. Communal parties spread that ideology more openly, while non-communal formations like Congress (I) do so under different disguises. The Congress in India has been resorting to different ways to appeal to the religious sentiments of the people in order to refurbish its shrinking electoral support during the past two and a half decades.

Till the end of the 1960s, the Congress depended upon the charisma of Jawaharlal Nehru and the legacy of the national movement to garner votes. After the death of Nehru, the Congress did not have a leader of the same stature who could arouse the national nostalgia of the freedom struggle.

Thus, devoid of popular symbols, Indira Gandhi resorted to populist slogans and measures like bank nationalism, the abolition of privy purses and 'garibi hathao'. But the appeal of these slogans and programmes was shortlived. Faced with political upheaval after the Bangladesh war, and failure of the family planning programme, Indira Gandhi lost her electoral base among the minorities, especially Muslims.

In the post-emergency period when the Congress returned to

power in 1980 with a greatly reduced majority, the Muslims did not vote for it during this election. Therefore, faced with an electoral debacle, the Congress sought to overcome the crisis by manipulating Hindu religious sentiments to its advantage. Mrs. Gandhi's policy underwent a major change as she became unsure of the Muslim votes and tried to woo the middle class Hindus.

The first major manifestation of this trend was the Hindu Kalash Yatra. By openly blessing and supporting the Yatra, Indira Gandhi tried to identify herself with Hinduism, it was an initial step. Ektamatayagna and Ektamata Yatra was organised by the Vishwa Hindu Parishad soon after some poor Hindus of Meenakshipuram were converted to Islam and both the BJP and the VHP raised a hue and cry over it. This raised the temperature of Hindu communalism in the country. The VHP jumped into the fray and launched an aggressive campaign against the conversion. Mrs. Gandhi used the VHP to promote her agenda among the Hindus.

She also accentuated the Punjab problem and Sikh militancy in order to win Hindu sympathy. She used Bhindrawale in Punjab to systematically encroach on the traditional vote bank of the Jan Sangh. In fact, it was the beginning of a new phase of dissemination of Hindu nationalism. The potential strength of religious appeal was exploited very soon for electoral purposes. Punjab and Jammu & Kashmir are the only explicit instances of communal politics to which the Congress had succumbed.

Mrs. Gandhi was unfortunately assassinated by her bodyguards and this was followed by anti-Sikh riots in Delhi and several places in north India. It was alleged that mostly Congressmen were involved in these riots. It was again a major communal catastrophe for the country. The Indian mainstream polity was now being communalised and thus the new phase of communalism began.

At the same time, a suggestion by the government to introduce the common civil code following an *obiter dicta* in a Supreme Court judgement brought out a great deal of Muslim resentment. The Supreme Court decided the case of maintenance (Shah Bano) for a divorced wife in her favour under Section 125 of the criminal procedure code. This was construed by the Muslim leadership as interference in the Shariah law and the Shariah law being divine could not be changed or interfered with. The government initially seemed to be in favour of a common civil code, then for electoral reasons it prevaricated and finally capitulated in favour of not disturbing the Muslim personal law.

Debate over the whole issue became communally coloured and secularists were ignored. The BJP fully exploited the passage of the bill by the parliament as an act of appeasement of Muslims. The Hindu middle class was easily convinced and began to support the BJP demand for a common civil code. Thus the common civil code became an important item on the Hindutva agenda.

When the Muslim Women's Bill was passed by Rajiv Gandhi's government, as a balancing act this government struck a deal with Hindu fundamentalists and the subsequent court order came to unlock the Babri Masjid which had been sealed by the administration many years earlier on account of a previous dispute. This was claimed as a victory by the Hindus, this also led to the heightening of tensions between the two communities. In 1984, the Ramjanaki rath was taken out in procession over various parts of north India as a part of the Ram Janambhoomi Andolan for the "liberation" of Lord Rama's birthplace from the hands of Muslims.

The Congress (I) Party increasingly fell back on religion for electoral games. This only provided additional nutrients to the soil for breeding Hindu communalism. The BJP saw great prospects for coming to power through elections to become a decisive political force within the Indian state. The BJP worked hard to consolidate its mass base among the middle class Hindus. The party appears to believe that Hindu nationalism has gripped the consciousness of a large proportion of the masses and therefore it must make use of every available opportunity to fertilise the soil, letting the concept (Hindutva) take deeper roots. The BJP, with the help of medieval history, created an atmosphere of animosity between the two communities, holding Muslims responsible for capturing it in the past.

The Ram Janambhoomi movement was fundamentally political in character. They further intensified the Ramjanam Bhoomi movement by announcing the Rath Yatra, which turned into, as the newspapers put it, 'Blood Yatra'. A large number of communal riots broke out all over the country on account of the demolition of the Babri Masjid. December 6, 1992 resulted in widespread communal violence in Bombay, Surat, Ahmedabad, Kanpur, Delhi, Calcutta and Patna. No history of communal violence in India can ignore this catastrophe; it was a clever ploy by the BJP to increase its strength in Parliament at the cost of thousands of human lives. The Sangh Parivar's ideology has been based right from the beginning on hatred and violence. It remained unchecked because of the soft policies of the state. The BJP took political mileage out of this and when it came to power it tried to consolidate its Hindu vote bank both in urban and rural India.

The communalisation of civil society was spreading faster under the NDA government led by the BJP. In order to spread Hindutva, it started to capture democratic institutions. It systematically reconstituted the committees of various research institutes like ICHR, NCERT and important educational institutes. It not only captured the political and social sphere but allowed the Sangh ideologues to monopolise not only educational and cultural institutes but also helped them to consolidate their roots in rural areas by sending their 'pracharaks' to spread the ideology of Hindutva. Secular space in the field of education and culture is of vital importance for the unity and integrity of India. The BJP propaganda easily caught on and began to pay rich political dividends. This whetted its appetite for political power. Thus the decades of the 1980s was the most dangerous decade in which not only did the Nehruvian concept of secularism begin to be questioned but the communal forces succeeded in consolidating their political base.

The new phase of communalism which started in the 1980s is based on the fact that people are more vulnerable today to the ideology of communalism mainly because religion provides all the inputs for intensifying hatred. Thus the idea of vengeance against that sacrilege becomes sanctified as a virtue. Communalism as an ideology has become institutionalised in India through political behaviour, the formal system of education, the media, communal riots and the acts of various components of the state. That is the socio-cultural environment in which the newly formed perception of religious identity among large sections of the urban affluent has intensified communal consciousness. It may be an earlier coincidence in time, but the new phase of communalism in India has evolved almost during the same period when consumer revolution and stock market revolution have been ushered in by state policy, and the BJP, despite all its religious loyalty to religion-bound tradition, is a staunch advocate of a comprehensive economic policy which can only spread consumerism.

Communalism has also made deep inroads into the consciousness of rural areas. In fact, earlier it was believed that communalism is an urban phenomenon, but the Gujarat riots have broken this myth and proved that forces of Hindutva have been successful in creating their stronghold in rural India as well. In fact, the Gujarat carnage proved that one should not underestimate the potentiality of communal forces for occasionally whipping up communal frenzy which itself spreads communalist consciousness. The pressing need today is to evolve ways and means to intervene with a view of stemming the rapid communalisation and prevent further polarisation of society which was a result of communal mobilisation since the new phase of communalism. Indian society has been completely communalised and polarised after the Gujarat episode. In fact, Ashish Nandy, in one of his articles on the Gujarat violence, has pointed out that India has experienced partition twice. In 1947, it experienced the partition of the geographical territories and in February 2002, during the Gujarat violence it experienced the partition of minds thus polarising the two communities forever.

Still, a major strength of Indian tradition is its composite character developed through religious interaction and synthesis. The theological discussions and debates in which scholars of all religions, whether Hindu, Christian or Islam have participated and enriched our knowledge and intellectual tradition.

Communalists are using the past (history) for their own political agenda. Secularists can use the cultural synthesis approach to counter communal focus. In fact, local-level secular activities are very important to struggle against communalism. We need neighbourhood communities to check the growth of ghettoisation and stop further polarisation of Indian society. The neighbourhood communities formed on the basis of cutting across identities of caste and religion. We need to construct conciousness on the basis of secular issues and secular ideas. These communities could be nodal points of anti-communal consciousness as well as the organisational network to resist the quest of communalism to acquire power.

Today communalism is primarily an instrument for acquiring power. And power is, to begin with, acquired at the grassroots level and therefore it has got to be contested at that level. These local associations or grassroot communities are a way of positing an alternative to communalism. This should be one of the tasks for combating communalism today and since communalism has to be fought on a long-term basis, it is necessary to develop an organisational network. The secular space has to be widened as it has shrunk in the past few years. In fact, to widen the base of secularism, the campaign against communalism needs to be treated as a struggle for changing the minds of the people — decommunalising them. The anti-communal struggle is a negative struggle. It is a struggle which tries to evolve ways and means to oppose communal propaganda. We have to transform our struggle against communalism into a struggle for secularism. Such a struggle can be meaningful only if it is part of a struggle for a humane society —a society in which human beings are recognised and respected as citizens of the nation, not on the basis of their being 'Hindu', 'Muslim', 'Christian' or 'Sikh'. It can be successful if we integrate this struggle of secularism with the larger struggle for a just society. Therefore, under the present conditions of heightened communal conflict, when both communities are poles apart, an indifferent civil society has to convert into a vibrant civil society because we cannot leave our children's future at stake. We have to come out of the era of darkness and accept that multicultural societies can only progress once they move towards a cultural synthesis and issues of citizenship replace issues of communalism.

To understand the phenomenon of communalism we have to adopt an integrated approach and evolve a methodology which takes into account medieval history, British rule, the freedom struggle genesis of communalism in the post-Independence period, the new phase of communalism in the 1980s, communalism to fascism in the 21st century, polarisation of communities and the role of indifferent civil society. It is only integrated understanding of communal violence that will enable us to understand and find a remedy.

My analysis and presentation of the issues in the communalisation of Indian society is not a new addition to already existing material on communalism. In fact, the observations made by me have been made much more ably by Dr. Asghar Ali Engineer, Prof. K.N. Panikkar, Prof. Paul Brass, Prof. Mushirul Hasan and Prof. Imtiaz Ahmad. Even my analogy on politicisation of religion and criminalisation of politics has been made earlier by Prof. Rajni Kothari, Prof. Atul Kohli and Dr. Asghar Ali Engineer.

The merit of my study lies, however, in its comprehensiveness and its attempt to analyse communalism since its genesis to institutionalisation in Indian society. I have tried to critically understand not only the meaning and nature of communalism but an attempt has been made to understand different phases of communalism through an integrated approach. Given the political importance of communalism and its use as a political weapon with dangerous social and political implications, the need is not merely to understand the phenomenon to acquire greater clarity but also to evolve perspectives to counter and combat it. My efforts to critically examine communalism have brought out clearly the soft role played by the state. Since the inception of the new phase of communalism in the 1980s, we have noticed that the state has been party to communal events. In fact, communalisation of state institutions is the major reason for the shrinking secular space and communalisation of Indian society.

The basic question this book is concerned about is: what is the meaning and causation of communalism, and trying to understand and answer this question. Is communalism a static phenomenon, or is it something which has changed over a period of time? Is communalism of the pre-Independence time the same as communalism today or is it in its myriad and complex expressions the same in different parts of the country? These questions are important and answers to them have to be sought in actual manifestations of the phenomenon. Since these are not simple questions to answer, this study is only a preliminary attempt.

To undertake this study several people have helped me; first and foremost I express my sincere gratitude to Prof. Imtiaz Ahmad for taking time from his busy schedule to write a foreword for this book.

I have frequently discussed with him various issues and questions that confused and troubled me. He made extremely valuable comments, suggestions and criticism. His clarity regarding the subject facilitated my work. I am profoundly grateful to him for not only writing the foreword for the book but also for his interest, support and guidance.

In the same breath I wish to express my indebtedness to Prof. Anand Kumar for going through the manuscript and making patient, perceptive suggestions and criticisms of various parts of the manuscript. I was especially touched by the painstaking way in which he has corrected the manuscript.

I am grateful to all my colleagues at the Department of Sociology and particularly Prof. Mohini Anjum, Ms. Sheena Jain, Dr. Manisha Pandey and Prof. Tulsi Patel from the University of Delhi who were perennial sources of encouragement and inspiration.

The final stages of preparing the manuscript saw debts of a different nature though of no less importance. Thus thanks are due to my parents-in-law Mrs. Amina Khatoon and Mr. Haji Mohammad Ayub. Their affection and prayers were a source of immense moral support for me. I take this opportunity to acknowledge the affectionate support and contribution provided in their own way by my students Imtiaz Ansari, Iram Naaz and Indira Mishra to help me to complete my work.

Above all, I would like to thank my sons Rushan and Rubban for bearing with me during my long working hours. Words would be too inadequate to acknowledge the emotional support and encouragement provided by my husband Aijaz Ansari. His constant inspiration has helped me to bring this volume to print.

Arvinder A. Ansari

INTRODUCTION

India is a land of endless and limitless diversities. It is a land of people of different religions—Hindus, Muslims, Christians, Sikhs, Buddhists, Jains and others. India is inhabited with people speaking about 1,652 languages. About three mother tongues are spoken by over a lakh of people. There are about twenty-two literatures, it is a mosaic of different sects, castes and sub-castes, different regions and sub-regions, different foods, habits, traditions, manners, styles, fashions, dances, flora and fauna. The most salient feature of Indian history is the unity in diversity where different diversities co-exist. The strength of India lies in its diversities. It has strength of tolerance, cooperation and mutual confidence. It is the strength of the composite culture—a common heritage of India which strengthens Indianness and unity of the people. Indian society is based on the amalgamation and synthesis of different diversities and there is growth of pluralistic polity.

Social group conflicts and tensions are common to all human societies formed of a composite culture. Plural societies do face national problems of racial groups or minorities. India being a plural society has serious national problems, namely communalism which broadly means conflict between Hindus and Muslims, both being the two important components of pluralistic Indian society. Communalism has its genesis in modern India which was crystallised during the colonial period by the British into India and Pakistan in 1947. With partition the Muslim League, who played a retrogressive role got Pakistan, and it was believed that in the absence of the British government India would emerge strong, united, powerful and there would be no communal holocaust.

After sixty-five years of India's independence the sinister forces of fundamentalism, terrorism, casteism, regionalism and sub-regionalism, linguism, tribalism, obscurantism, and diehard rapid communalism have threatened and posed a dangerous challenge to national integrity and Indianness and the secular character of Indian polity is under siege as darkness is gathering on her horizon.

Religion, which does not preach animosity and stands for love and sacrifice, has been so exploited by the communal ideologues, political parties and organisations that it has become the major cause of communal carnage, fratricidal conflicts, bloodshed, loot, arson, butchering, gunning down, roasting and burning alive innocent men, women and children.

Secular values and the ethos of our polity enshrined in the Constitution are being eroded and the ideology of communalism is penetrating slowly and gradually into our political and social systems since India became free. The slogans of 'Hindu Rashtra', 'Muslim India', 'Khalistan', 'Christianistism', and the like are echoed by diehard communalists, communal ideologues and religious zealots.

Etymology of the Term Communalism

It is interesting to note that communalism as a term used in the social connotation of religious and racial antagonism especially in India, entered the English lexicon at about the same time, i.e. the mid-19th century, when the British Crown became the imperial soverign.[1] This simultaneity is not a mere coincidence. It establishes on the one hand a causality link between its occurrence in history and etymology and on the other, an organic link between the role of imperialism and the rise of communalism in India (not that communities in the same religious sense did not exist earlier nor that antagonism between them was completely absent). The pertinent point is that in the activisation of this very antagonism and its transformation from a latent inward-looking religious cleavage into the most articulate socio-political decisive conflict the presence and policy of British imperialism played a decisive role.[2]

Communalism as a term, and as a process requires certain clarification. Its literal, dictionary meaning, obviously reflecting Western usage, particularly British and American is at variance with its connotation in the Indian context. It is not a variance of 'kind' but of degree—'communal', 'communalist', communalism', are terms of approbation in the Western meaning of the term.[3] Indeed there is a basic contradiction in the positive and laudatory meaning given to the term in the European-American usage and the exclusively negative and pejorative construction put on the word in what is historically called the Indian subcontinent. In some English dictionaries it is amusing and amazing for us in India to read that 'communalism' is even a synonym of 'communism'! A 'communalist' in traditional English usage is thus a person of altruistic compassion attached to his commune or community, a person of deep social impulses and humanism identified with larger societal goals and community interest. In Roget's Thesaurus, for instance, the only inclusion of communalism is with the main synonym 'participation' which then includes other analogous terms like communism, collectivism, socialism and cooperation.[4]

But in India this positive connotation has acquired the peculiar meaning of animosity between Hindus and Muslims and now it also covers animosity between Sikhs and Hindus, communalism as a phenomenon has two different aspects.

(a) The material substratum of the phenomenon which consists of historical differences and disabilities—economic, social, matrimonial, cultural, educational, recreational, occupational and political among people inhabiting the same locality in India, arising out of and in turn accentuated by past and present laws, customs and traditions tending to foster exclusiveness, antagonism and estrangement between persons belonging to different religious and racial groups; and

(b) The manipulation, exploitation and regeneration of this substratum by interested elements such as :

> *(i)* foreign imperialists, *(ii)* the ruling party of the day *(iii)* economic and social vested interests *(iv)* employers of labour for anti-union and strike breaking purposes *(v)* anti-social elements tax evaders, corrupt elements, thugs and gangsters, and *(vi)* irresponsible demagogues, agitators and politicians.[5]

The proposition that communalism is the single biggest subversive ideology in contemporary India has been widely discussed. Quite often communalism is wrongly used as a synonym for religion or religious fundamentalism or conservatism and obscurantism or simply for a sense of belonging to a community. Synonyms sometimes confuse a 'part' for the whole and a also gloss over the nuances and specific and total character of communalism. **What is communalism?** Adherence to religion and religious system is not communalism. Attachment to a religious community or religiosity is not communalism. Exploitation of religion is communalism. Using a religious community against other communities and against nations is communalism. Affiliation to any social, cultural and service organ of a religious community may also not be communalism. (But restructuring one's sympathy, helping social obligations and range of services as citizens of a secular republic to the community of one's birth can be communalism).

These are merely irrational, unscientific and primordial orientations, due to conformism to traditions or because of fear of unknown and unbounded ambition. Even commitment to conservative values in social life and conservative orientation in politics is not communalism. It can be called social backwardness and political reaction. However, it should be recognised that all these aspects can be inputs for development of communal consciousness and indeed the communalists in various permutations and combinations have used most of these aspects in order to build their communal political base.

But "communalism" as a specific phenomenon in Indian polity is something different and more specific. Communalism is basically an ideology of political allegiance to a religious community as a primary and decisive group in the polity, and for political action. Communalism is a modern phenomenon, not a phenomenon of the medieval past. It is a sectarian, restrictive and negative response to the process of modernisation and modern nation building.

Communalism envisages a religious community alone as a base and universe of its political ambition and action. For a communalist, religious community is the only relevant and valid category in politics and in state affairs, and for the perception, analysis and reconstruction of a socio-cultural environment for a communalist a political system and its sub-system, like a party system and state craft, can and should be structured on the recognition of religious communities, as the foundational, grassroot and operational reality. Communalism is perception of other religious communities as inimical entities within a polity and within a nation, arranged in an unfriendly, antagonistic and belligerent equation one to another. Therefore the aim of communalism is politicisation of a religious community, which in turn will lead to communalisation of the political and social system.

It is necessary at this moment to define term 'communal' and communalism for minimising the interference of the otherwise existing ambiguities and contradictions that one encounters while studying social phenomena of this nature. A few attempts made ahead need to be reviewed for establishing some more clarity about the word 'communalism', it is that a multifactoral and complex social phenomenon like communalism cannot be explained or solved with the help of "single cause" thesis. This also does not warrant an exercise in mere accumulation of all the available information and details on riots. The causes of communal violence must be logically ordered and meaningfully arranged for proper interpretation. Now we shall review such efforts. Bipin Chandra, an eminent scholar of the subject in the context of modern Indian history views communalism as follows:

"Communalism is the belief that because a group of people follow a particular religion they have, as a result common social, political, economic and culture interests... In India (there are) different and distinct communities which are independently and separately structured or consolidated that all the followers of a religion share not only a commonality of religious interests but also common social interests, that is, economic, political and cultural interests... Religion has to become the basis of their basic social identity and determinant to their basic social relationships and they possess an inherent tendency to act and function as a separate group or entity or unit in these fields".[6]

Harbans Mukhia states that communalism is the phenomenon of religious differences between groups often leading to tension and even rioting between them. In its not so violent manifestation, communalism amounts to discrimination against a religious group in matters of employment or education. The locus of communalism is placed at the point of tension either in the form of discrimination or in the extreme form of a riot. But tension/riot is merely an overt manifestation of a phenomenon which also manifested itself at its other end in a silent, almost imperceptible form and the two together consitute a spectrum in which communalism could get expressed at any point.[7]

Similarly, Smith defines communalism in India, "as the ideology which has emphasised as the social, political and economic unit the group adherents of each religion and has emphasised the distinction even the antagonism between such groups".[8]

Smith further states that the problem of communalism "has not remained constant and unchanged has grown and shifted, changed and developed and is till changing and will continue to develop".[9]

Imtiaz Ahmad has raised a few propositions on this theme. According to him, "the character and nature of communalism is keenly changing. Communal riots reflect this in terms of internal shifts in the nature, orientation and location." The communal tensions do not reflect the systemic breakdown as believed but they are indicators of the onset of dynamic and secular changes as a result of economic development. According to him they are also not a set of "illogical and irrational actions". They are essentially a consequence of "deeper social processes at work" which produces not only communal but several kinds of social and civil tensions and conflicts. Communal tension and riots are only a part of such a phenomenon. He says that sociologically communal rioting is a clearly directed, goal-oriented social action whose logic and rationality is clear to those who engage in it".[10]

In brief, communalism has been studied through various perspectives. There exist multiple diverse perspectives to analyse the phenomenon of communalism which are discussed in detail in Chapter One, "Communalism: Through Various Perspectives". In this chapter an attempt has been made to incorporate the various perspectives of communalism. Communalism is not only a religio-cultural phenomenon but an expression of a struggle for the fulfilment of politico-economic ambitions of elite of respective communities.

In Chapter Two entitled "Social Interaction Among Hindus and Muslims: Pre-Independence Period", an attempt has been made to study the history of communalism from the medieval period to modern (1857-1947). The aim of this chapter is to discuss the genesis of communalism, its crystallisation in modern India through various stages. All the important events which led to the formulation of communalism have been discussed.

Chapter Three, "Changing Orientation of State" deals with the period after 1967-87. After 1967 there was a serious shift in the political system of India. Division in Congress led to serious change in our political system which was also reflected in the socio-economic system of our society. Since the 1970s, due to decay in the democratic institutions of the state, some serious fissiparous tendencies crept into our political and social system.

Chapter Four, "Communal Violence and State", focuses on the alarming increase in the growth of communal violence, which is a manifestion of long-lasting, persistent and continuous activities of communal politics organised, promoted, controlled and used by the middle classes, politico-bureaucratic and small industrial business elites and landlords from each community. Through these sections, the ideology speaks into and lends expression in the available political arena at local or supra local level.

Chapter Five, "Communalism to Fascism", focuses on analysing the Gujarat riots of 2002, since the Gujarat carnage is unprecedented in the history of communal violence in post-independent India. Never before has such communal carnage taken place not even before Independence. The violence unleashed with state complicity and support of the ruling party has permanently fragmented the process of communal harmony. In fact it was a fatal attack on the plural ethos of our society and final step towards the polarisation of civil society. Therefore, in this chapter an effort has been made to analyse the causes of polarisation and an attempt has been made to discuss the role of vibrant civil society to arrest the growth of ghettoisation and polarisation.

REFERENCES

1. Ramji Lal (ed.), *The Communal Problem in India: A Symposium,* Karnal: Dayal Singh College Publications, 1988, p. 7.
2. Ibid., p. 10.
3. R.C. Dutt (ed.), *Challenge to the Polity: Communalism, Casteism and Economic Challenges*, Delhi: Lancer Publications, 1989, p. 20.
4. Rasheeduddin Khan, "Understanding India's Communal Politics", *Mainstream,* Vol. 7, No. 26, March 1, 1969, pp. 10-11.
5. K.B. Krishna, *The Problem of Minorities or Communal Representation in India,* London: George Allen & Unwin Ltd, 1939, p. 356.
6. Bipan Chandra, *Communalism in Modern India,* New Delhi: Vikas Publishing House, 1984, p. 1.
7. Harbans Mukhia, "Communalism and Indian Politics", *Economic and Political Weekly*, Vol. 18, No. 39 (September 24, 1983), p. 1664.
8. Wilfred Cantwell Smith, *Modern Islam in India: A Social Analysis,* Delhi: Usha Publications, 1979, p. 187.
9. Ibid., p. 190.
10. Imtiaz Ahmad, "Political Economy of Communalism in Contemporary India", *Economic and Political Weekly,* Vol. 19, No. 22/23 (June 2-9,1984), pp. 903-906.

1

COMMUNALISM: THROUGH VARIOUS PERSPECTIVES

Communalism, regionalism and casteism have become closely linked with India's socio-political evolution and are today considered in-built negative slants in the contemporary Indian political and social system. With growing awareness and self-assertion among minority groups and a gradual federalisation process, these idioms have become significant indicators of our socio-political infrastructure.

Historically, communalism has its inception in the pre-British and British raj. But communalism in the present era has become a multidimensional phenomenon. In order to analyse communalism in the contemporary context, one requires an in-depth understanding of the social structure and social process of Indian society. In the interest of a proper comprehension of Indian communalism it is essential that we put it in the perspective of the present-day Indian situation. Such an approach would perhaps provide some new insights into our understanding of communalism. But before we analyse the theory of communalism and its overtones in the contemporary context of Indian social realities, let us see how communalism has been conceptualised in our literature of political science and sociology.

Scholars on communalism agree that communalism is an Indian phenomenon and it is distinct from racism and racial conflicts. The distinctiveness lies in the fact that it does not have its roots in biological factors; it is an acquired trait. It pertains to any of the racial or religious communities specially of India. "Communalism in effect represents some material differences and disabilities such as economic, social, matrimonial, cultural, educational and political. These attributes of communal groups are manipulated or exploited by political parties and economic and social vested interests."[1]

In recent years, particularly after India's independence, several studies have been undertaken on the problem and ramifications of communalism. These studies have revealed that the problem of communalism may be approached differently through various perspectives.

Minority-Majority Perspective

The treatment of the communal problem as a minority-majority syndrome was done by theorists of democracy. According to Humayun Kabir, "Democracy is a necessary precondition for the emergence of the minority problem."[2] To him, there was no clear-cut existence of minority before the advent of democracy and the consequent birth of democratic institutions and decentralisation of power, diversification of interest groups, elite contest and minority consciousness against the majority rule.[3]

Humayun Kabir has felt that "the fact of minority consciousness has caused cleavages and political rifts between several minority groups, more particularly between Hindus and Muslims in India.[4] Some empirical studies on voting behaviour and election campaigns have shown that nomination and election of candidates have been largely influenced by minority-majority consciousness. The votes have been cast and mobilised on the basis of identity.

This particular approach of minority-majority relationship has focused its attention on two major facts. One, why do communal conflicts pertain to the Hindu majority and Muslim minority? Two, why are Muslims rather than any other religious minority in India so conscious of their grievances? (Though the situation has changed since the last two decades, Sikhs and Christians are also emerging as vociferous minorities.)

It is true that minority consciousness has been dominant

among Muslims since pre-Partition days due to the deliberately devised divisionist policy of the British, arousing political aspirations among the Muslims of India. Second, Muslims who had a dominant status before the entry of the British in India, find it hard to digest that they have been brought down from master status to subordinate status. Third, the most important fact which has made Muslims more identity conscious and their minority character, is that after the division of the subcontinent, they are looked down upon as traitors, who are disloyal to their motherland. The discriminatory attitude of the majority has further alienated the Muslims from the mainstream.

The Muslim minority consciousness is also attributed to the practice of Hindu revivalism which has encouraged the Muslim minority to organise on a communal basis and once some Muslims did so, Hindu revivalism added fuel to the fire which in turn reinforced Muslim activity. Similarly, the Hindu agitation for the adoption of the Nagri script agitated the Muslims to resent it. Hindu campaigns for Hindu Universities encouraged Muslims to demand a Muslim one and Hindu opposition to a separate electorate for Muslims only made Muslims demand it more rigorously.[5] Hindu-Muslim revivalism as an action and reaction syndrome solidified majority-minority consciousness.

According to this perspective, Hindu-Muslim or Majority-Minority consciousness has a vital component in the growth of communalism in India and in this regard three important points have been analysed by the adherents of this pespective.[6]

1. The Muslim minority feels neglected at the hands of the Hindu majority.
2. Hindu-Muslim mistrust has generated a feeling of fear and prejudices between the two communities.
3. Government's policy of appeasing the minorities has encouraged the latter to assert their demands at times unreasonably.

The 'Minority-Majority perspective' to study communalism in the post-Independence period has its limitations. It is true that the minority consciousness in India is spreading out having both implicit and explicit ramifications, but it would be a mistake to identify the communalism of the Muslim minority as being directed against the Hindu majority. If the problem is viewed in the narrow perspective, there appears little chance of its resolution. The conception of minority will become dormant as the nation-building process makes progress.[7]

Such an approach implies that if minorities give up their separatist and communal attitudes the problem will be solved. It suggests that minority groups being sub-cultural enclaves in society are typical, hence in order to maintain structural balance they need to be integrated into the mainstream of society either through an acculturation or assimilation. This approach takes very little account of the problems having deeper roots. It does not go into the basic structural factors associated with communalism.

Further, understanding the problem from the minority-majority situation becomes unscientific and biased. For a while, the total community can face certain common problems like fear of majority. For instance, it is widely differentiated in economic classes. Political orientation and issues, language, culture of the Muslims as a whole cannot be viewed as uniform. As a result the problems of Muslims taken by these writers are not of the whole community but only of upper class Muslims. Representation in government service, legislature and parliament is the problem of the minor section among the Muslims. Religious dogmatism, conservatism and communal identification on the basis is again the field of a small section of Muslim leadership that tries to keep itself in power and works for its interests through the exploitation of communal loyalities.[8] The biggest flaw with this approach is the tendency in the literature on political development and modernisation to focus on 'National Integration' as a process of state building and to treat all the other loyalties except those of the state as 'parochial or primordial loyalties', divisive in their impact and detrimental to national integration. Thus, focus on national integration, as Paul Brass writes, has "resulted both in ideological and analytical implications and consequences, ideologically such an approach has fostered an exaltation of the contemporary nation state and downgrading of ethnic values."[9]

Analytically, it appears that national orientation is a simplistic concept to apply to the predominantly multi-ethnic state of India. It is not only, as Paul Brass writes, that "Inter-ethnic relations become more important to the integrative process than the elite-mass relation in such a state but that the process by which intermediary loyalties are developed are largely ignored in this approach."[10] The vertical and horizontal division of the Indian social structure shows that both the terms 'majority' and 'minority' are imprecise—there is no homogeneous oppressor majority which exploits minorities.

Plurality and Ethnicity Perspective

Originally the term 'plural society'[11] denoted Asian countries characterised by collections of communities linked together by the commerce and plantation economics of the colonial regime. Today it refers to nations characterised by a plurality of cultural institutions which are held together by a dominant community by political arrangements which are coercive in their implications.

A group on some basis or other has a sense of belongingness and this sense distinguishes it from the inhabitants of the area where their minority functions. Ratna Naidu observes a rising tide of identity aspirations. She suggests "that there is more to communalism than class struggle. Along with being a struggle for class interest it is also a kind of ethnic conflict that is to say an understanding of communalism and this separation is an ethnic separation since it is the ethnic identity which provides meaning to personal interests."[12]

The word ethnic is used to refer to any group having a common historical heritage, anything which binds people together into a community which also means sharing a cluster of beliefs and values. One value held in common by a number of persons is insufficient to sustain an ethnic community. One may give the example of Muslims, while circumstances and cluster of values bound them together into a community vis-à-vis the Hindus, other circumstances and other cluster of values split them later into Punjabi and Bengali and such other communal factions.[13] Ratna Naidu says that the present tension is "ethnic and communal in a broader sense than merely religious or social"[14], which is a product of the political process of modern times. This politicisation has taken place not on any single polarised issue but multiple community criteria issues.

The caste and communal organisations are considered essential to developing nationhood in a pluralistic society. Commenting on the role of ethnicity in Indian politics, Paul Brass argued:

> "There is nothing false about the consciousness that develops around the choice of ethnicity, as the identification that best serves the interests of the ethnic group. It often works in both the short and the long run and it sometimes also leads to creation of solidarities that cut across the internal class division within the ethnic group. It works because among other things it is easier to organise small culturally distinct groups than large multicultural class collectivities and because admittedly state authorities would rather recognise cultural categories than class categories."

Brass further says,

> "It boils down to the simple fact that people pursue their interest in society by forming groups and selecting identification that maximise their advantage in the competition for scarce jobs and economic resources and for political power."[15]

As postulated by Naidu, ethnic conflict is responsible for communal conflict, can be explained through Schemerhorn's[16] model of centrepetal and centrifugal force.

1. **Differential:** Comprising two or more different units having different rights ranging from high and low.
2. **Equivalent:** Comprising different units as exclusive corporate groups with equivalent standing in the society as a whole.
3. **Uniform:** Which multiplies ethnic membership as a pre-requisite for political activity and includes all in the universal category of citizenship. New pona in India we see all three modes ranging from ancient (caste), British (separate representation) and independent India (equal

citizenship). Now to see the third model which is prevailing today is important. Although Gandhi and a few other nationalists fought for the new dispensation, the egalitarian ideal imbedded in it violates the cultural norm of hierarchy presupposed in the caste system. Still people are divided in regard to region, religion, language, etc.[17]

Schemerhorn has analysed ethnic relations first by classifying ethnic minority groups into types and second by enlarging the scope of exploration to the "study of total societies". He has got five inter-group sequences.[18]

1. The Emergence of Pariah: under this comes Scheduled Caste.
2. Emergence of Indigenous Isolates: comprising Scheduled Tribes.
3. Religious cleavages: comprising Jains, Sikhs.
4. Colonisation or Conquest: this comprises Muslims, Christians and Anglo-Indians.
5. Migration, bygone and recent: comprising Jews, Parsis, Chinese.

Now one has to see to what extent these minorities of different categories are integrated into the national life. By integration he means "a process whereby units of elements of society are brought into an active and coordinated compliance with the ongoing activities and objectives of the dominant group in that society."[19] Every minority has either close relations with the dominant group and acceptance of its standards, or other form of relations separate from the dominant group, which can be either physical or cultural, a centrifugal goal. The crucial point here is the behaviour that is in agreement and disagreement of the dominant group—which he has tried to explain through a centripetal and centrifugal paradigm which will analyse all sorts of relationships of the minority and majority.[20]

Jains fall in the centripetal model because they follow the pattern of assimilation and incorporation. Under the centrifugal category come Parsis, Jews and Christians. Under this model the dominant group recognises the autonomy and the distinct character of the group. The plurality of the culture is sanctioned by the majority.

Now comes the minority who are in disagreement with the dominant group in its mode of affiliation. It will assume one of two types—the first is where the subordinate seek some kind of assimilation in dominant groups but are denied it, which is forced segregation with resistance under which falls the scheduled caste. Second is forced assimilation by the dominant group, under which mode the minority wants to preserve its distinctive way of life and culture but is forced by the dominant group to accept the prevalent customs, that is, forced assimilation with resistance. Under this category fall Anglo-Indians, Scheduled Tribes, Muslims and Sikhs.[21]

However, explaining thc whole conflict on the basis of ethnicity is not feasible. This whole paradigm is more easily understood when seen in the perspective of other institutions working horizontally. On the vertical level we can divide people among different communities but again the same communities are divided horizontally in different classes. In the present atmosphere of scarcity, politicisation of grievances by the leaders of different groups take place. People who in real means suffer and face poverty tend to cling to their own community, for they feel that their own community will be beneficial for them.[22]

Again, we can't say that if we do away with plurality we won't face any conflict. First of all it is practically impossible to have a non-plural society. Society is formed by individuals and one cannot negate the concept of individual differences based upon race, sect, culture, etc. There will be several other kinds of differences, which are used as tools by the superior class to garb the scarce resources. There will be discrimination based on extraneous elements. Thus basically it is exploitation manifested in the shape of religion, culture, language and regional conflict. [23]

Some theorists believe that it is not the ethnic groups but their operation in the socio-economic life of the nation that generates an area of conflict and disharmony. It is not religion but the plural character of society and the feudal nature of the state that produces communalism. P.C. Aggarwal's[24] study of the

Islamic revivalism among the Meoes suggests that a democratic political system hardens the lines which divide religious and ethnic groups. These, collectively consolidated appear more advantageous for political gains. "All these movements which assume a religious cloak have economic causes."[25]

The Indian bourgeoisie is not sufficiently revolutionary to fight feudalism and it remains to strive for a rational secular ideology. The compromising position of the ruling class is evident in all matters of culture, religion, education and so on. The point is that the real beneficiaries of the systems are the metropolitan bourgeoisie, monopoly bourgeoisie and the landlord. Such a system hastens the process of pauperisation of the people and is the greatest source of disruption and disintegration in the polity. It produces uneven economic development and fosters agitations like the one in Assam.[26]

The pluralist approach based on the one-nation theory recognises the existence of various minorities, linguistic and cultural groups. The advocates of the pluralist approach believe in protective discrimination as a positive attempt to uplift the lowest of the low in the society. The pluralist theory recognises the minority group or communities but cannot solve their genuine cultural problem. In a non-socialist underdeveloped country like ours, this theory fails to satisfy the aspirations of the minority groups. The ruling party which subscribes to this theory cannot adopt a genuine secular position since it is concerned with appeasing the religious sentiments of the majority for giving the obvious political benefit.[27] Thus the question is not whether India is one nation, assimilating people speaking different languages, living in different areas and belonging to different ethnic, cultural groups or whether there should be biological fusion of different communities, but "connection with the nature of the socio-economic order." Socio-economic policies of the system lead to concentration of power and deny equality of opportunity to the majority of the people belonging to all communities, so in that case disregard and disharmony are inevitable. In such a system the ruling class has a vested interest in dividing people along communal and religious lines."[28]

Another factor related with the cleavages on religious lines is the politicisation of this natural likeness having strong emotional appeal. Distinction on any grounds especially on religious grounds is used as a tool for political gain. This is one explanation of communalism and the main proponent of this theory is Prabha Dixit.[29] According to her, when one community decides to put political demand on the basis of religio-cultural differences then community consciousness becomes a political theory in a communal form. Political autonomy is declared as a condition of cultural autonomy. In a plural society, social tension and conflict are actually power conflicts among different groups. Giving the base of religion on the theoretical level to this conflict is the essence of communalism in the form of political viewpoint. Communalism in the form of political fact emerged in the 19th century. Cultural identity is never dangerous unless it is mingled with political identity.[30]

Communalism is not a religious phenomenon because from the angle of socio-political relationship, the area of conflict was confined to the ruling class only. Basically it was a struggle for power, and there are many instances when Mughal rulers took the help of Rajputs and Shivaji had Muslim fighter brigades and Muslim generals. Prabha Dixit says, "it was not the result of religious hostility between the Hindus and Muslims, it was evolved as a political doctrine and was closely associated with the struggle for power."[31]

Proving the point that communalism is a tool in the hands of the ruling party for their own vested interests, N.C. Saxena says, "There seems to be a positive correlation between the period of intense rioting and deterioration of the relationship between the top political leaders of the two communities."[32]

Communal Consciousness: Traditional Perspective

The adherents of this approach consider that the religious and cultural differences among the two communities, i.e. Hindus and Muslims was the main factor that led to the growth of communalism. According to them religion and culture was a factor which is the cause of antagonism and mistrust between Hindus and Muslims.

Some research studies of that time have evidence which shows that both the communities were equally traditionalist and conservative. Although the popular belief at that time was that Hindus were keen on modernisation and change, studies carried out regarding the issue have shown that both communities responded to modernisation, change and development as long as it did not come in the way of their religious beliefs. It is true that Muslims became more conscious of their identity owing to the policies followed by the British. The urge for the preservation of a distinct religious identity became stronger among Muslims because of their mistrust in the majority community, which also led to the backwardness of Muslims because they could not rationalise the fruits and benefits of change and reform at that time.[33]

This peculiar attitude of Muslims was due to the reason that they were looked down on as traitors who were disloyal to mother India. They were never accepted as the "sons of the soil" and prejudice and biases in the majority community raised consciousness among the Muslims to maintain and preserve their distinct identity more vehemently. They felt insecure in terms of life and property and had a fear psychosis that the majority community wanted them to abandon their distinctiveness and cultural identity, as the majority tried to maintain consciously the position of pre-eminence over the Muslims.[34]

There appears to be a vertical lack of communication between the two communities, both are non-receptive of secular ideas and both practise religion with rigidity even at the cost of nation-building. Religious rigidity is emphasised by the elites of both the communities. The elites on the basis of religion are able to mobilise and consolidate their respective communities because religion acts as a cementing force in inter-religious conflict. It helps elites to muster support in the name of religion to pursue their selfish interests which in the real sense are non-religious. In the name of religion and tradition they are able to push back the forces of modernisation and change, which lead to enlightenment and awareness.[35] Studies conducted to analyse election behaviour of the people have shown that religion acts as a powerful source in the nomination and selection of candidates.

In the post-Independence era, a large number of communal organisations of both the Hindus and Muslims became active and effective. Communal leadership thus made its headway, blurring the chances of rapid growth of the Muslim community accepted the leadership of the Ulema, which was dogmatic, anti-secular and anti-democratic. Muslim Ulemas as well as Hindu Pandits remained unconcerned towards the growing schism and pursued vested religious interests without caring for communal outbursts.[36]

Leaders of the Jamat-e-Ulema Hind state, "we had made a positive contribution and played a constructive role during the pre-Independence period. Somehow we have moved close to the goals of the Jamaat-i-Islami which stands committed to theocratic rule based on the shariat."[37] The Muslim-majlis-e-Mushawarat which had considerable influence among Indian Muslims had started playing a fanatic role like some Hindu organisations who claimed to be safeguards of Hinduism such as the Hindu Mahasabha, Vishwa Hindu Parishad, RSS, Bajrang Dal, Shiv Sena and have led to Hindu fundamentalism.[38] The biggest folly of these organisations is that they try to assert Hindu culture even on non-Hindus. They have also tried to bring them under the fold of Hinduism but are mistaken because forced assimilation leads to segregation.

They insist that "the minorities are expected to imbibe Hindu ways, defer to Hindu gods and goddesses, accept Shivaji and Maharana Pratap as their heroes and decry Aurangzeb and bigoted Muslim rulers".[39] Politicisation of religion in the post-Independence period has led to severe consequences as had the search for cultural independence. The search for cultural identity and distinctiveness has further alienated communities, and the chances of integration, modernisation, development have suffered at the hands of narrow-minded religious leaders and politicians, who for their own petty selfish interests had given rise to this social tension.

The supporters of this approach by and large seem correct when they say that religion is both a cementing and a divisive force. It is a cementing force in intra-community matters and it becomes divisive when the matter relates to inter-community affairs. This approach also has its own limitations. Adherents of this approach treat religion completely separate from socio-economic and political forces operating in our social system. It treats religion as the soul force in the rise of communalism. History is repeated with evidence of both communities in spite of their religious differences having lived in harmony during all periods of Indian history.[40] Critics of this approach hold the view that in the post-Independence era politics has cut across religious differences rather than the other way round. Communal riots in this period are constructed and are the handiwork of politically motivated aspirants. Religion is used as an instrument to mobilise the communities on communal lines.

Communalism: Historical Perspective

Much of the work done on communalism in the post-Independence period, that is till the previous decade has an historical explanation of the phenomenon. Historians tend to view the communal problem in Indian history as the problem of political relations between Hindus and Muslims. With this viewpoint in mind, the theorists of this particular stream try to locate the causes which contribute to their growing eastrangement from the beginning of the 19th century.[41] History reveals that communal riots are not a product of a day nor an outcome of a particular event but have a determined historical evolution. These factors, history indicates, pertain to the presence of mutual animosities, distrust and prejudices. An analysis of communal riots both in the past and the recent years shows that communal outbursts have often taken place whenever religious festivals of the two communities have occurred on the same dates (Holi and Eid or Dusshera and Mohurram) or whenever religious symbols or scriptures are dishonoured. History also indicates that the change of the government or political system has not helped in changing communal behaviour. History, therefore, explains that communal behaviour is not restricted to certain periods or situations but has been a continuous phenomenon.

There has been relatively little actual comparative work in history in India, historians usually tending to confine themselves to the study of a single society. Occasionally the confinement is not merely to a particular society, but also to a specific period in the history of that society.[42] The perspective of historians remains limited due to the constraints of methodology and information, their source of information is basically documents and archival records which are scattered, scarce and incomplete most of the time. They have to collect, organise and correlate their evidence plate by plate from different archives and it normally takes them years of patient and careful scanning of documentary evidence before they can reconstruct a sufficiently reliable picture of a social phenomenon.

Most of the historians who have dealt with communalism in the recent past have taken into consideration the modern period and have focused their attention exclusively on the relationship between Hindus and Muslims, neglecting to trace the structural behaviour and social system in the society.[43] History is an explanatory discipline and the orientation of the historians is descriptive. Therefore, they have hardly studied the communal problem as a problem for investigation in itself. It has been studied as an aspect of the national movement. Most of the historians tend to view communalism as a deviation from nationalism and set out to view the causes which contributed to this deviation. For that matter, even those few historians who have studied communalism as an object of study in itself have unconsciously been led to think that communalism represented deviation from the national movement.[44]

Given this unconscious bias among our historians, the communal problem in India has been seen only in terms of political conflict between Hindus and Muslims. Since the communal problem has been viewed as a problem of political relations between Hindus and Muslims alone, our explanations of it have been somewhat superficial. Most historians have put forward either simple psychological, cultural or historical explanations for the communal problems rather than explaining it in terms of the structural features of the society within which the conflict between Hindus and Muslims occurred and crystallised.[45] Psychological explanation tends to see the conflict as a kind of frenzy and ignores the deeper social and economic conditions responsible for its emergence.

The cultural-historical explanation describes it as: (i) the lasting heterogeneity between Hindus and Muslims; (ii) that the pattern of interaction and relation between the two communities and their access to power before and during British rule; (iii) the nature and content of the national movement which is alleged to be either strongly underscored by Hindu sentiments or secular; (iv) the relative backwardness of the Muslims and their reluctance to benefit from cultural and social reforms in the 19th century; (v) preservation of separatist identity as the religious community by the Muslims and their aspirations for political dominance.[46]

Communal Consciousness: Socio-Economic Perspective

The other major current of opinion about communalism is the socialist, therefore, socio-economic approach. W.C. Smith[47] probably just sketched the social roots of the communal phenomenon and suggested that there was something more to it than mere religious differences. Thus communalism is "that ideology, which emphasises at the social, political and economic unit of group, of adherents of each religion and emphasised the distinction even the antagonism between such groups."[48] Despite the formation of Pakistan, the communal problem remained unsolved, indicating that there was something radically wrong with the two-nation theory and provided the impetus for the re-examination of the hitherto accepted popular explanation of Hindu-Muslim relations. On the one hand, elements of communalism in the writing of Indian history were identified and on the other hand, analysis laying stress on unreal elements of the social structure, elements which could be identified with the non-progressive section of the society like the communal pattern were ignored if not exactly rejected.

Historians such as Irfan Habib interpreted the history of India preceding the British conquest with the avowed purpose of showing that all previous governments had been despotic and monstrously cruel. Communal interpretation of Indian society led to the formation of two schools of Indian historians, viz. Ishtiaque Hussain from Pakistan and R.C. Majumdar from India who are the exponents of these schools.[49] Bipan Chandra, citing the example of communalisation of Indian history, writes that we consider Shivaji, Rana Pratap, and Guru Gobind Singh as the heroes on the ground that they fought against the Mughal rulers. He poses the question that on what ground can these struggles be called national struggles.[50]

Numerous historians have written about the false interpretation of history on communal lines. This sensitivity of scholars to the dialectical naturalist approach to historical studies focused attention on the role of the social class. The result was the work of Sumit Sarkar's, *Swadeshi Movement in Bengal 1905-1906*, Mushirul Hasan's *Nationalism and Communal Politics in India 1916-1928*, Bipan Chandra's *Communalism in Modern India*, Asghar Ali Engineer's immense literature on communalism such as *Communalism and Communal Violence in India*; *Socio-Economic Bases of Communalism; Communalism in India* and many more. Ideas which Jawaharlal Nehru expressed over five decades ago when confronted with the reality of increasing communalisation of Indian politics, had come of age.[51]

Socialists have claimed to strike at the basic root and give a new definition of communalism—explaining communalism as by and large a struggle for power and an economic problem and poverty of masses being divided into religious categories. Hitherto studies were explaining the mobilising aspect that is consciousness from above but the question arises why religious cleavages could be used for communal mobilisation. Asghar Ali Engineer answers this question thus: "Caste hierarchy in functional terms certainly had greater social acceptability as a religious category. Thus socio-economic issues projected in religious idiom acquire an emotional base around which communal polarisation then occurs."[52]

Sudhir Kakkar[54] has emphasised this aspect "how, by taking birth in a particular community, a child is socialised in that atmosphere and he assimilates unconsciously or subconsciously the beliefs, values, etc. of that community." He points out the subservience of the child and later, the adult to the family group, a subservience in which the individual's own 'normative identity does not exist independently, but only in relation to his primary group of social milieu. This primordial tie without being used as a tool, plays an important role in generating conflict. Key complexes of religious beliefs with their organising symbol are thus implanted during the pre-reflective years of childhood. Thus, this normal affinity works at the consciousness level for religious exclusiveness and in forming communal identities but these identities gather struggle when they come into the wider social, political and economic arena. Because of these, the normal feeling in its pathological form gets religious roots though actually it is somewhat detached from religion.

All the above factors can help to explain the reasons of conflict between Hindus and Muslims in the 19th century, but these causes fail to explain why Hindus and Muslims remained socially distinct, separate, advocating different political positions, neither do they explain why this antagonism existed and how it crystallised.

The re-emergence of communalism in spite of the secular outlook of the Constitution calls for re-examining the communal problem from the wider perspective, adopting a comparative approach which takes into consideration the process of social interaction. We have seen the whole development of the phenomenon along religious, political, historical, social and economic lines. If we move from this synchronic to a diachronic level of analysis, we find the whole phenomenon existing in a continuous normal to pathological level. At the normal level it is the likeness, on the same basis or the other to a particular community or unity which a person belongs to. This sense of unity distinguished him from the other community. This explains the question why interests in conflicts are subsumed under the communal phenomenon perceived by actors in terms of antagonistic relations among different communities. The base to understand communalism lies in coming to terms with the unconscious process of social integration.[53]

REFERENCES

1. Richard Lambert, "Anti-Muslim Attitude of Hindu Communal Groups", in Richard L. Park and Irene Tinker (eds.), *Leadership*

and Political Institutions in India, Princeton: Princeton University Press, 1959, p. 6.

2. Humayun Kabir, *Minorities in a Democracy,* Calcutta: Firma K.L. Mukhopadhyay, 1968, p. 6.
3. Ibid., p. 8.
4. Ibid., p. 80.
5. Francis Robinson, *Separatism Among Indian Muslims: The Politics of the United Provinces' Muslims, 1860-1923*, Cambridge: Cambridge University Press, 1974, p. 349.
6. A.G. Noorani, "The Grievances of Indian Muslims", *Secular Democracy,* August 1969, p. 31.
7. A.B. Shah, "The Facts of Communalism", *The Secularist,* No. 8, December 1970, p. 48.
8. K.L. Gauba, *Passive Voices: A Penetrating Study of Muslims in India,* New Delhi: Sterling Publishers, 1973, pp. 27-28.
9. Paul R. Brass, *Language, Religion and Politics in Northern India,* Cambridge: Cambridge University Press, 1974, p. 5.
10. Ibid., p. 6.
11. J.S. Fernival, *Colonial Policy and Practice: A Comparative Study of Burma and Netherlands,* Cambridge: Cambridge University Press, 1948, p. 172.
12. Ratna Naidu, *Communal Edge to Plural Society: India and Malaysia,* New Delhi: Vikas Publishing House, 1980, p. 11.
13. T.N. Madan, "The Dialects of Ethnic and National Boundaries in the Evolution of Bangladesh", in Navlakha, S. (ed.), *Studies in Asian Social Development,* New Delhi: Vikas Publishing House, 1974.
14. Ratna Naidu, op. cit., p. 14.
15. Paul R. Brass, "Review: Class, Ethnic Group and Party in Indian Politics", *World Politics,* Vol. 33, No. 3, April 1981, p. 453.
16. R.A. Schermerhorn, *Ethnic Plurality in India,* Tucson: University of Arizona Press, 1978, p. 369.
17. Louis Dumont, "Nationalism and Communalism", *Contributions to Indian Sociology,* Vol. 7, March 1964, p. 50.
18. Schermerhorn, op. cit., p. 21.
19. Ibid., p. 24.
20. Ratna Naidu, op. cit., p. 43.
21. Louis Dumont, op. cit., p. 45.
22. Prabha Dixit, *Communalism: A Struggle for Power*, Delhi: Orient Longman, 1974, p. 96.
23. Schermerhorn, op. cit., p. 79.

24. P.C. Aggarwal, "Islamic Revival in Modern India: The Case of the Meos", *Economic and Political Weekly,* Vol. 4, No. 2, October 18, 1969, pp. 1677-1681.
25. Karl Marx and F. Engels, *Pre-Capitalist Socio-Economic Formations: A Collection,* Moscow: Progress Publishers, 1976, p. 483.
26. Prabha Dixit, op. cit., pp. 102-108.
27. Moin Shakir, "On National Integration", *Social Scientist,* Vol. 10, No. 4, April, 1982, pp. 36-45.
28. Ibid., p. 38.
29. Prabha Dixit, op. cit., p. 112.
30. Ibid., p. 123.
31. Prabha Dixit, op. cit., p. 76.
32. N.C. Saxena, "The Nature and Origin of Communal Riots in India", in A.A. Engineer (ed.), *Communal Riots in Post-Independence India,* Hyderabad: Sangam Books, 1984, p. 54.
33. Humayun Kabir, op. cit., p. 72.
34. Rasheeduddin Khan, "Understanding India's Communal Politics", *Mainstream,* Vol. 7, No. 26, March 1, 1969, pp. 10-11.
35. Zenab Banu, *Politics of Communalism: A Political-Historical Analysis of Communal Riots in Post-Independence India with Special Reference to the Gujarat and Rajasthan Riots*, Bombay: Popular Prakashan, 1989, pp. 11, 13.
36. Ibid., p. 20.
37. Girilal Jain, "The Communal Problem", *The Times of India,* October 16, 1974.
38. Krishna Gopal, "Communal Issue Revisited", *The Times of India,* October 10, 1974.
39. Girilal Jain, op. cit.
40. Moin Shakir, *Muslims in Free India,* New Delhi: Kalamkar Prakashan, 1972, p. 81.
41. Imtiaz Ahmad, "Perspective of Communal Problem", in A.A. Engineer (ed.), *Communalism in Post-Independence India,* Hyderabad: Sangam Books, 1984.
42. Ibid., p. 136.
43. Ibid., pp. 136-137.
44. Ibid., p. 137.
45. C.M. Jain and C.L. Sharma, "Communal Economy and the Problems of Governmental Control", *The Indian Political Science Review,* Vol. 5, No. 2, April-September, 1971, p. 128.

46. Imtiaz Ahmad, op. cit., p. 134.
47. W.C. Smith, *Modern Islam in India: A Social Analysis*, New Delhi: Usha Publications, 1979, p. 185.
48. W.C. Smith, op. cit., p. 186.
49. (i) R. Thapar, H. Mukhia, and Bipan Chandra, *Communalism and the Writing of Indian History,* Delhi: People's Publishing House, 1969.
50. Bipan Chandra, "Communalism in Retrospect", *Mainstream,* Vol. XXI, No. 45, July 9, 1983, pp. 8-15.
51. Jawaharlal Nehru, *Selected Works of Jawaharlal Nehru,* Vol. VI, New Delhi: Orient Longman, p. 43.
52. A.A. Engineer, "Socio-Economic Basis of Communalism", *Mainstream*, Vol. 21, No. 45, July 9, 1983, pp. 15-18.
53. Sudhir Kakkar, *The Inner World: Psychoanalytic Study of Childhood and Society in India,* New Delhi: Oxford University Press, 1978, pp. 103-117.

2

SOCIAL INTERACTION AMONG HINDUS AND MUSLIMS: PRE-INDEPENDENCE PERIOD

Communalism has been with us for about a century now, and considering the trend of social and political development, it appears that we will have to live with it for quite some time to come. Is communalism inherent in Indian society? We would have to probe into the historical past, particularly the centuries of Hindu-Muslim interaction and encounter. But there are not many accounts of social relations between Hindus and Muslims in the medieval period at many levels that will throw light on this aspect. Therefore, we have to draw our conclusion from the nature of the Muslim State in India and the attitudes of Muslim Sultans towards the Hindus, in order to gauge the level of Hindu-Muslim relations. One should also examine the factors that contributed in the 4th and 6th centuries to the development of communal consciousness resulting in the partition of India in 1947 on the basis of religious identities.

India is a heterogeneous society. Class, caste, culture and regionalism divide the upper and lower classes of each community. Communal consciousness, usually found among the ruling elite, was inspired more by political expedience than by religious sentiment in medieval India but manipulation of religious sentiment became a prominent feature only in British India. In this chapter an attempt has been made to see how communalism was nurtured on the soil of the Indian subcontinent. The growth of communalism can be divided into three phases of Indian history: the medieval phase, the British phase and the post-Independence phase. The categorisation of phases has been done with the main purpose of examining the gradual growth of communalism in different periods of Indian history. The chapter mainly relates to the rise and growth of communalism between the Hindus and Muslims in two phases of history; viz. medieval phase and the British phase.

Our objective is to delineate the phenomenon of communalism as it existed in different phases of the political history of India. Here we may look for the origins of communalism in the social structures of two communities—Hindus and Muslims—in the medieval phase.

The Hindu social structure that existed in the medieval period may be characterised as a capsule which did not permit any mobility from lower caste to upper caste or from one caste to another. "The unchanging division of labour enforced under the varna-oriented caste system established a state or permanent pattern of income distribution. The tendency of immobility observed in the Hindu society resulted in the creation of the two classes—the elite and the masses."[1] The elite comprised the "twice-born" and some of the intermediary castes. The masses comprised the lower castes including the untouchables.

Hindu social structure, though divided vertically and horizontally, maintains its unity by socio-cultural and religious interaction. In fact, it was a conjunction of separate layers different from other strata of the society. The unity of the two diverse groups was retained by the concepts of purity, pollution and ritual ranking.

The Hindus had a tendency to assimilate alien groups into their fold through 'Sanskritisation'.[2] In the case of Muslim integration however, the process did not work for the Muslims because they were not willing to sacrifice their group identity and culture. The Muslim social structure had an inbuilt institutional framework which was immune to such integration.[3] Theoretically, Muslim society appears to be an open society. Islam does not recognise birth as the basis of social stratification. It rests on the assumption that access to political power and social eminence remains open to all its bona fide members. But the Muslim invaders, who made their entry into India and at a later stage stalled here, had a social stratification which was closed in character.[4]

An analysis of the Muslim social structure as found in the medieval period shows that the upper ranks, namely, the Ashraf, consisted of the original stock of Muslim immigrants, while the remaining two comprised converts from the lower caste groups. The Muslim elite had their distinct identity, and the lower groups originally members of the low-caste Hindus, had leanings towards the rituals and rites of the Hindu caste system. In Muslim society, therefore, at the elite level, there were sharp differences from the elite culture of the Hindus. At the lower levels of Muslim society, socio-cultural differences with the low-caste Hindus were marginal; the only differentiating mark between the groups was that of religion, one professing Islam, the other Hinduism. The Muslim elite groups occupied power positions as Sultan, Mansabdar, Wazir, etc. The lower categories of Muslims were engaged in the service of the upper ones and mainly worked as menials.[5] The distinct identity of the Muslim elite groups, which was virtually the ruling class, rested on an endogamous pattern of marriage and a separate and distinguishable way of life. The Ashrafs did not have any relations on a marital basis with the lower class Muslims. This set the ruling class apart from the lower ranks of Muslim society.[6]

The Muslims did not try to break the distinctness and divisions of Hindu society. On the other hand, the social equality practised by the Muslims was commendable, in the sense that Hindus were allowed to maintain their structure of the elite and the masses. In the matter of recruitment to the administrative services of the States the Muslim government took full cognizance of the caste factor, and high offices were exclusively conferred on the twice-born Hindus. "We do not find a single example where the Sultan or the Emperor appointed a low caste Hindu to any high office."[7] The Hindus, on their part, did not make efforts to develop communal politics by organising themselves as a strong force against the Muslims. The Hindu elites were opportunistic and pragmatic in their own fashion in ensuring their survival and maintaining their glory.[8]

In the 18th century political power rested with the Rajputs, Marathas and Jats. These groups never organised themselves or practised communal politics. If the Rajputs were fighting against the Muslims for maintaining their traditional elitism, the Marathas largely waged wars for financial reasons. The Marathas were ruthless fighters and for booty they did not hesitate to set village after village on fire, ruin crops and kill hundreds of innocent people.[9] They did not wage war against the Muslims on a communal basis. Broadly speaking, the Rajputs, the Jats and the Marathas in the latter period of Indian political history did not organise themselves to combat Muslims. Religion, which was a major differentiating factor between the Hindu and Muslim groups, never worked as a unifying force among the Hindus. The politics of war therefore, was strongly characterised by regional and caste considerations.[10]

This is evident from the simple fact that in no period of Indian history did the Rajputs, the Jats and the Marathas form any alliance to launch an organised struggle against the Muslims. On the other hand, they did not miss any opportunity to fight among themselves to gain financial or power super-ordination. A very significant point which deserves to be made in this context is that the Hindu power elite consisting of the Jats, Marathas and Rajputs, did not organise the vast Hindu masses in the fights that they put up against the Muslims. Largely, it seemed a power struggle of the upper groups of the Hindus in which the vast Hindu masses were not concerned.

The ruling class of Ashrafs in India tried to maintain its group identity by comprising or waging wars with the Hindu ruling class. The relationship between the two ruling classes was therefore, largely based on utilisation ends. It was eminently practical for a minority group such as the Muslim elite to have the cooperation and support of the local Hindu elite. If occasion so demanded, they entered into marriage alliances and political treaties. The relationship was essentially determined by the pressure of the politico-economic exigencies. Muslim liberalism in administration was based on political considerations.[11] The Muslim elite group never organised itself as a communal force or as a force having distinct religious and national identity. The wars waged by the Muslims during this period were non-communal and largely based on regional, non-religious and political considerations.[12]

The large masses among the Muslims remained isolated from the political bargains which the Muslim elite struck with the Hindu elite. The Muslim masses had no access to political power. They were denied any such opportunity because of their low origins and poor way of life. Socio-culturally, the Muslim masses were unorganised and were closer to the Hindu masses than the Muslim elite. The Muslim masses, like their Hindu counterparts were scattered over the thousands of villages of the country. At the village level, therefore, the Muslim and Hindu masses were almost on equal footing in terms of economic deprivation and socio-cultural manners. Indian society during the medieval period, broadly speaking, consisted of the Muslim elite, the Hindu elite and the Hindu-Muslim masses, the two being in contact on regional, economic, non-religious and non-communal considerations.[13]

In linking the above analysis with the total Indian social structure and with the 'politics of communalism' existing in the medieval period, it will be noticed that the elite groups of both the communities were effectively engaged in securing power. The Ashraf elite, on the one hand, wanted to give the culture of their parent countries a firm footing here, and on the other, took all precautions, structurally, to keep away from the local converted groups.[14] In order to retain their domination, they had struggles with the Hindu power groups frequently. Whenever there was a need to seek the cooperation and support of the masses they appealed to them on various pretexts, including the religious one. At no times, during the medieval period, did the Ashraf group make any attempt to foster unity among the Muslim masses or the groups of religion. In brief, the Muslim elite group had its own political and economic interests and these guided their behaviour with the Hindus.[15]

The Hindu social structure was dominated by its elite group, the Brahmins and Rajputs and, in the later period, the Marathas and Jats as well. The Hindu power elite, whether represented in the personality of Maharaja Rana Pratap or Shivaji, did not have national and communal considerations.[16] They fought with the Mughals, tooth and nail for their self-preservation. It was to maintain the glory of their caste and the glory of their kingdom that the reorganised Hindu masses, if part of the power struggle, were involved on communal and regional considerations.[17] The medieval period was thus characterised by a process of the formation of two distinct groups—Hindus and Muslims—on several considerations such as political, economic and others, but not communal. The Muslims, that is, the elite who were strangers to the country were not willing to integrate themselves in the mainstream of Hindus. Rather, they were engaged in strengthening their group identity. The Hindu elite were worried about the retention of their domination. Communalism, it is evident, did not raise its head during the medieval period.

During the medieval period, both the Muslim and Hindu elite had consolidated themselves and were struggling hard to establish dominance for their respective groups. The establishment of British rule was a new political force in the power struggle. The British first settled in Bengal. The political and administrative policies followed by them had a strong impact on the Muslim social structure, the British axe first fell on the Muslim elite group.[18] The Muslim elite were found mainly in the cities of Dacca, Murshidabad, Burdwan, Hooghly and Calcutta (now Kolkata). These Muslims had privileges by virtue of their administrative control over the provinces. Unlike the Hindu zamindars they did not have hereditary control over the land. Neither did they form a ruling group, whereas the Muslim rulers were to be superfluous between the actual revenue collector and government. When they became confident of their position they kept the Muslim rulers out. This deprived the Muslim elite of the economic resources derived as a ruling group.[19] Thus the deprivation of political power and consequent loss of economic resources relegated the Muslim elite to a difficult existence.

The Mutiny of 1857 is of historic importance to understand the genesis of communalism. The uprising of 1857 completed the ruination of the Muslim elite.[20] Power passed into the hands of the British Crown. The Mutiny made it very clear to the British that if Hindus and Muslims were united they could displace British rule in India. They were well aware of the caste, class, community, and composition of Indian society. So in order to establish a firm footing in India and tilt the balance of political power on their side, they adopted the policy of Divide and Rule, with which they had experimented already in their existing colonies. Under this divide and rule policy, the British tried to crystallise and accentuate the differences among these two communities in India. This followed a planned policy of concession and repression to control the political power of India.[21]

With the establishment of British supremacy, the Hindus and Muslims started drifting away from each other. This was due to the deliberate policy of conciliation and repression towards Hindus and Muslims. British consolidation of power in India was in two different perspectives. For most Hindus, it appeared to be transfer of political authority from an archaic to a modern set of foreign rulers.[22] The adjustment to the latter was deemed to be easier and considerably more desirable for reasons of future development. Thus the Hindus were relatively more prone to reconcile themselves to the new political system as well as to the general process of modernisation.[23] The British policy of appeasement towards Hindu was interpreted as a preferential treatment on the basis of religion. They started looking for a new ideology to unify and defend their community, and to concentrate on a religious plane. The then feudal influence of the great landowners, the Arya Samaj was founded in 1875 with its insistence on the unique and superior qualities of Hinduism.[24] The British followed the policy of repression towards Muslims during this period, because they suspected them to be the main culprits in instigating the Mutiny in 1857.

The intermediate Muslim class was adversely affected by the virtual takeover of Indian trade by the East India Company and the other British and European merchants. "The artisan class was exposed to a dual attack—one, by the vicious tariff policy followed by the British government in the early stages of the Industrial Revolution, and by the competition from factory-made goods after the Industrial Revolution. The result was the decline of Indian domestic industry and the impoverishment of the artisans, who were mostly Muslims."[25]

Muslims started to look upon the British as the usurpers of their political and economic strength. A feeling of humiliation and defeat persisted, especially among the Muslim aristocrats. Still having memories of the great days of the Mughal empire fresh in their minds, the Muslim experienced difficulty in adjusting to a minority status among a subject population.[26] The forces of modernisation released by Britain in the country adversely affected the Muslim community. Persian was replaced by Bengali and later on by English. The change was most unwelcome to the Muslim elite and they were deeply upset. British policy thus swung in favour of the Hindus both in the new system of education and the revenue system under the Permanent Settlement. This made Muslims conscious about their identity on the basis of religion and they grew apprehensive of Hindu domination and resented the tenacity with which the Hindus had advanced themselves in various spheres.[27] For the first time in the history of Muslim politics, the Muslim masses were politicised by their elites on a religious basis. The political alignment of Muslim politics was further strengthened and supported by the subversion of Muslim states all over the world like Arabia, Africa and Asia. The Muslim countries succumbed to the advance of the European powers, that is, Britain, France and Russia.[28]

The foundation of the Indian National Congress broke the political isolation of the two groups and put forward the ideology of nationhood, besides providing a political mechanism to fight against the foreign power. The Congress ideology of India as a nation did not appeal to the Muslim elite.[29] The Muslims were apprehensive about joining the Congress because it was formed by Hindus. They became anxious about their future. They felt that joining the Congress meant Hindu domination. The argument given by the Muslim elite was that the problems of Muslims were different from those of the Hindus. Muslims are economically backward and needed protection and patronage from the government. Describing the plight of the Indian Muslims, Sir Ameer Ali wrote, "the waves of adversity, which have one after another passed over the Muslim aristocracy have proved as injurious to the interest of the community as those of the state."[30]

Sir Syed also put forward the same argument when he urged the Muslims to concentrate on English education. His plea was that if they did not do so, they would not only remain a backward community but would sink lower and lower. His main concern was for the spread of English education among Muslims. With this end in view he worked hard for a reconciliation between the British Government and the Muslim upper middle class.[31] According to him, the object of the promotion of the Congress was that "the Government of India should be English in name only, and that internal rule of the country should be entirely in their own hands. What antagonised Sir Syed Ahmed was not the Congress and its leaders but the demands made by the Congress—its clamour for a system of representative institutional and facilities to Indians. He warned Muslims against accepting the Western representative system in India, which could mean their reduction to a position of permanent minority. In his speech in Lucknow in 1887, he said, "whatever the system of elections be adopted there will be four times as many Hindus as Muslims and all their demands will be gratified." Moreover, he feared that since the large community would override the interests of the smaller community, "the ignorant public would hold government responsible for introducing measures which might make the differences of race and creed more violent than ever."[32]

Sir Syed Ahmed in 1883 put forth the demand of nomination of members of the minority community and requested the government not to have wholly elected local bodies in a country having great difference in religion and language.[33] Syed Ahmed's aversion to Muslims joining the Indian National Congress further accentuated the communal divide.

The British imperialists followed the policy of "Divide and Rule." The Governor of Bombay, Lord Elphinston wrote, "Divide at Impera was the old Roman motto and it should be ours."[34] The policy manifested itself for the first time in the form of the division of Bengal. Viceroy Curzon announced the partition of Bengal in 1905 into the Muslim-dominated eastern and Hindu-dominated western parts, ostensibly in the name of administrative efficiency and convenience was a serious attempt by the British in the direction of crystallising the differences between the two communities. The manner in which partition was planned and the speeches made by Lord Curzon, the then Viceroy, reveal that the real motive behind it was to divide the people on the basis of religion and promote differences and antagonism between Hindus and Muslims.[35]

Right through the British period, the Muslim elite did their best to retain their traditional status. When the Congress began to work for democratic ideals along constitutional lines, the Muslim elite too decided to work on constitutional reforms.[36] As a part of this policy decision, delegation of prominent Muslims led by the Agha Khan, met the Viceroy at Shimla on October 1, 1906 and demanded definite constitutional safeguards to protect the exclusive interests of the Muslim minority. One of the demands was the grant of separate Muslim representation in all the elected bodies, beginning from municipal boards to the Imperial Legislative Council. It was a charter of demands for special privileges for Muslims.[37]

The Shimla deputation was deliberately engineered; it well suited the British administrative policy. The British wanted to combat the rising tide of nationalism kindled by the Indian National Congress. Imperialism and Muslim communalism shared a common interest in hampering the national movement.[38]

The Muslim leaders who were present at Shimla also felt the need to have a political organisation of their own, with a view to safeguarding the interests of their community. The first concrete step was taken by Nawab Salimullah Khan of Dacca, who proposed the scheme for "the Muslim All India Confederacy"[39], the aims of which would be to support the government and protect the interests of the Muslims. This was also to aim at countering the increasing influence of the Congress and to impress upon the

Muslims not to join that body. Thus on December 30, 1906, the Muslim League was formed under the Presidentship of Sir Syed Ali Imam. He emphasised and talked about historical separateness of the Muslims in terms of nationality, character and creed. He held the Indian National Congress responsible for the birth of an independent All-India Muslim Political Organisation.[40] The following were the aims and objectives of the League:

(a) To promote feeling of loyalty towards the British Government among the Muslims of India and to remove any misconception that might arise as to the intention of the government with regard to any of its measures.

(b) To protect and advance the political rights and interests of the Muslims of India and to respectfully represent their needs and aspirations to the government.

(c) To prevent the rise among Muslims, of any feeling of hostility towards other communities without prejudice to the other aforementioned objectives of the League.[41]

Separate Electorates

According to the Morley-Minto Reforms of 1909 and Montague-Chelmsford Reforms of 1919, a fixed number of seats was allotted to each minority and special electorates were assigned to each. The scheme encouraged not only Muslims but other groups also to consider themselves as national units with their particular interests separate from the interests of the general body of Indians. Nothing could be a more efficacious method of fractionalising the country and preventing the growth of the consciousness of nationality. This vicious principle was given the widest extension possible to make the working of responsible government almost impossible.[42]

The Lucknow Pact (1916)

The outbreak of the First World War in August 1914 brought the Muslim League closer to the Congress. During 1915 the combined efforts of Jinnah and Wazir Hasan on the side of the League and Annie Besant on the Congress accelerated reconciliation between Hindus and Muslims.[43]

At the two joint meetings of the Congress and League reform committees at Lucknow in 1916, the Congress accepted the demands for separate electorates and also agreed to cooperate with the Muslim League for demanding weightage to Muslims in all those provinces where Muslims were in a minority.

Under the Congress-League scheme, Muslims got over-representation in the provincial legislatures in Bihar, Bombay, Madras and Central Provinces. Being aware of the dominant position of the Muslims in Uttar Pradesh,[44] they were given thirty per cent of the seats there. The price paid for these concessions was that the principle of weightage to the minority community was also applied to Bengal and the Punjab, reducing Muslim representation in the provincial Legislative Councils from fifty-five per cent to fifty per cent in the Punjab and to forty per cent in Bengal.[45] The Congress gave formal recognition to communal politics in India as it had consented to recognise the All-India Muslim League as the mouthpiece of the Muslims and also accept separate electorates.

Given the large-scale Muslim discontent over the Khilafat question, M.K. Gandhi seized the opportunity of championing the cause of Muslims in order to win their confidence and enlist their support for the freedom movement. He called **Khilafat, "the kamadhenu",** as it was for him "an opportunity of uniting Hindus and Muslims, as would not arise in a hundred years.[46] On his advice, the Muslims decided at a meeting held on December 22, 1919 in Delhi to withhold all cooperation from the government if the British Cabinet did not revise the Turkish Peace Terms. An all-parties conference was held in Allahabad which decided upon the policy of non-cooperation and appointed a committee consisting of Gandhi, the Ali brothers, Azad, Kitchlew, Hasrat Mohani and Haji Ahmad to draw up a programme. On August 1, the Khilafat Committee entrusted Gandhi with the leadership of the Non-cooperation programmes for the redress of the Khilafat and Punjab wrongs and the achievement of Swaraj.[47]

Non-cooperation and the Khilafat Movement was the last instance of a combined Hindu-Muslim challenge to the British. Between 1919 and 1924 there was complete unity between Hindus and Muslims. The Muslims had pursued their objective with the full concurrence of the Congress, though the main purpose of the latter was enlisting their support in the nationalist movement. But the suspension of the civil disobedience movement in 1922, and the abolition of the Caliphate in 1924, left the Muslims high and dry. Indeed there was a feeling of frustration among both Hindus and Muslims many of whom now turned towards communalism. The Hindu-Muslim unity was based on a fragile foundation; anti-British sentiment had brought the two communities together but with the collapse of the non-cooperation movement, communal harmony was over.[48]

Religious Revivalism in 1924

The Hindu and Muslim religious revivalism movement tended to consolidate the two communities into two all-India groups, comprising and uniting the multiplicity of smaller regional and cultural sections which existed independently in the Middle Ages. This process of internal communal integration made a marked advance during the 19th century. The other process of political integration of the communities into a national united advanced *pari passu*.[49] The highly emotional and romantic religious upsurge of the second half of the 19th century directed minds into religious channels which slackened the vigour of the secular national movement.[50]

The Shuddhi and Sangathan movements were started among the Hindus and the Tabligh and Tanzim among the Muslims. In the first place, the aim was the recovery of the community's past greatness. History reminded them that their ancestors had built vast empires, made glorious contributions to the advancement of culture and played an unforgettable role in world affairs. In the second place, compared to their past, their present appeared humiliating and shameful. They had lost their independence, the pride and pomp of their states had been trampled into dust by alien races. Their industry was destroyed, their people impoverished, their upper classes reduced to helpless beggary for the small favours of their masters. Their moral stature was stunted and spirit dwarfed. Consequently, they desired to bury as quickly as possible the hateful present and emerge into a new and more spacious way of living.[51]

Religious revivalism led to the crystallisation of community in the rigid sense of the word.[52] As a result the Hindus began to think and speak of Hindu nationalism and the Muslims of Islamic nationalism, and thus the foundations of a two-nation theory were laid. It did not occur to the protagonists of the theory that the term Hindu or Muslim nationalism is self-contradictory; nation is a purely territorial, secular and political concept and religion, race and language have no necessary relevance to it. It was not difficult therefore for the British to use the cultural and religious differences between the Hindus and Muslims for their imperial political purposes. The lure of office and patronage was stronger than the appeal of nascent nationalism which summoned Indians to suffering and sacrificing but promised no rewards in the immediate future.[53]

Communal Violence 1923-30

This particular period of the British era was marked with intensive communal violence. It started with the Moplah Rebellion, which intensified animosity between the two communities. Data available shows that this period witnessed more serious riots than at any other time in history.

Serious riots occurred in Amritsar, Multan in Punjab. In the same year violence broke out in Meerut, Moradabad, Allahabad and Ajmer. The most serious of these disturbances occurred at Saharanpur in connection with the Moharrum festival. In September 1924 very serious rioting took place in Kohat (now in Pakistan) in which 155 persons were killed and more than Rupees nine lakh properties of both communities were looted. The whole Hindu community of Kohat had to evacuate. Gandhiji undertook a fast in Mohammad Ali's house at Delhi for Hindu-Muslim amity. But these riots which were the handiwork of a third party had done their task, they had created an unbridgeable gap between the two communities.[54]

Communal Representation and Round Table Conferences 1930-32

The British government's intention to promote communalism was apparent at the time of the Round Table Conference for which delegates were chosen on the basis of their communal leanings. The refusal of the Congress to participate in the first session of the Round Table Conference, consequent on its involvement in the civil disobedience movement strengthened the position of the Hindu Mahasabha there and gave it further opportunity to maintain its intransigence on the communal problem. Despite the willingness of the Hindu representatives of the Liberal federation to satisfy some of the demands of the Muslims, it stuck to its guns with the result that no progress could be made towards resolving the communal deadlock.[55]

As a result of the Gandhi-Irwin truce, Gandhi attended the second session of the Round Table Conference (1931) but his presence did not provide any solution of the communal problems any more. Non-fulfilment of their (Muslim) demands produced much greater reaction among the Muslim leaders and made them turn to the government for the satisfaction of their demands.[56]

Communal Award 1932

After the failure of the Round Table Conference, Ramsay McDonald, the British Prime Minister, as Chairman of the Minorities Sub-Committee released the Communal Award accepting, not only the Muslim communal demands but further pushing the depressed class towards communalism by introducing separate electorates for them. To appease the Muslims, Viceroy Lord Willingdon even agreed to give one-third share to make Sind a separate province much before the Unity Conference finalised its recommendations.[57]

The Communal Award was based on the British theory that India was not a nation but a congregation of racial, religious and cultural groups, castes and interests. Morley and Minto in 1909, Montague and Chelmsford in 1919 and the Simon Commission in their report of 1930 built the structure of the Indian society on communal lines.[58]

No greater disservice could have been done to India's aspiration for independence than the decision of McDonald on the communal problem. Separate representation was provided not only for Muslims, but for the Sikhs. The Anglo-Indians, the Indian Christians and the depressed classes, as well as for Europeans, landholders, commerce and industry.

Introduction of the Communal Award had serious repercussions on Indian society because differences which were at social, economic and religious levels and were diffused now became political differences which were widened by the separate elections and which sowed the seed of communalism in our society.[60]

The plan obviously took for granted that the programmes and parties in India at the centre and in the provinces would be determined not by economic, political and social considerations but on the basis of religious and communal interests. Therefore, from the foundation, the entire structure of constituencies, elections and ministers were organised on communal lines.[61]

Separate electorates led to consequences which destroyed the solidarity and vigour of the state. As the existence of the state depends on a fundamental agreement among the common constituents of society, any measure which weakens the will to agree is harmful. But separate Hindu and Muslim electorates deprived the communities of mutual obligation and minimised the opportunities of agreement.[62]

Introduction of this system was motivated by evil intentions and was maintained in order to effectuate imperialist designs. It was bound to produce evil results. Its maleficence proved incurable because the attempts of the two communities chiefly concerned to come to a settlement were thwarted by the existence of a third party—an alien factor in the body politic.[63] Even the British felt and knew that division of society on the basis of caste and community would prove hazardous for the future of India.

The Montague-Chelmsford Report was quite categorical on the question of communal electorates. They wrote, "we conclude unhesitatingly that the history of self-government among the nations who developed it and spread it through the world is decisively against the admission by the state of any divided allegiance against the state's arranging its members in any way which encourages them to think of themselves primarily as citizens of any smaller unit than itself.''[64] Oliver, Ex. Secretary of State, wrote in *Contemporary Review:*

"The system of communal representation is a disastrous expedient bound to be fatal to the satisfactory working of any constitution that embodies it. It is an obvious and admitted fact, that the existence of the communal electoral system now aggravates and exacerbates communal rivalries and hostilities between Indians whose political interests, in all matters falling within the sphere of the mechanism of the government are independent of creed. Moreover, the expedient is in itself ineffective.''[65]

As a result of the Act of 1935, Provincial Assembly elections were held in 1937, and the Congress commanded a majority in the Legislative Assemblies of six out of eleven provinces.[66] Its position in the country thus became quite strong and formidable. In contrast, the performance of the Muslim League was not at all impressive. It had won only 109 out of 482 seats contested. Besides, it also failed to win a majority of seats in any of the four Muslim-majority provinces.[67] The results created despair among the League's leaders as all their calculations had proved wrong. They had contested the elections in the hope that as a result of the Communal Award, they would be able to have full sway over the majority provinces, but now this hope was dashed to the ground.

With the Muslim League's failure to form a ministry in any province except in Bengal, the former started spreading communal viruses in every nook and corner of Muslim habitation. The Muslim League claimed that in Congress-ruled provinces Muslim life, limb and property had been lost and mosques defiled. The Muslim League depicted the Congress as a Hindu communal body and spearheaded the two-nation theory.[68]

Muslim communalism passed through eventful phases during this period. On October 17, 1937, the League changed its demand in its charter from "full responsible government" to "full independence." A year later, on October 10, 1938, with Jinnah in the chair, the Sindh Provincial League passed a resolution saying that in order to maintain peace in the Indian subcontinent it was essential to safeguard the interest of the Muslim minorities. In order to ensure economic and social betterment and political self-determination, the country should be dismembered into two nations, for the Hindus and the Muslims: "that we divide into two federations, namely, the federation of Muslim states and the federation of non-Muslim States."[69]

The Cripps Mission in March 1942 gave an indirect recognition to the Muslim claim for a separate homeland made in the Lahore Resolution, 1940. It was an incentive to the Muslims and made them more enthusiastic to achieve their goal as the idea of Pakistan which till then had remained in the realm of fancy acquired the shape of a viable proposition.[70]

The Quit India Movement launched by Gandhi and the Congress hardened the attitude of the imperialist government; which not only suppressed the Congress ruthlessly but also went out of its way to secure the help of the Muslim League and raise the image and position of Jinnah.

Jinnah's negative approach and intransigence was upheld by the British even in 1945 when in the Wavell offer, an attempt was made to form a new Executive Council by including equal proportions of caste Hindus and Muslims. At this time also, the Imperial Government preferred to rely solely on the communal card. Documents of the 'Transfer of Power' contain a revealing picture of the British Government's endeavours to placate Jinnah's communalism.[71]

Once again during the Cabinet Mission period it was revealed that the British did not take a stand to avert the deadlock between the League and the Congress because of the vacillating attitude of the Viceroy resulting from his old prejudices against the Congress and the sympathies of a section of the British bureaucracy in India and conservative party at home with the League.[72]

Throughout the proceedings of the Mission, the Viceroy had leanings towards the Muslim League. He even threatened the

Congress that he would not convene the Constituent Assembly without the participation of the League.[73]

The communal attitude of the Hindus and the Muslims and the support rendered to it by the British reached its tragic culmination in the partition of the country. One wonders whether it has really served the purpose or solved the problems or fulfilled the aims and aspirations of the two communities.[74] The answer perhaps is no, as this is amply proved and evidenced by the presence of the communal monster in contemporary times.

Our objective in analysing the socio-political scene from the medieval period to the dawn of the British regime was to explore the causal forces determining the socio-political structure of communalism. In doing so, we have tried to analyse various events to track the forces which led to communalism. To recapitulate, in the medieval period the Muslims were struggling only to establish their identity as an immigrant group settled in a foreign country. Mainly, the elite group was faced with this problem for lower sections of the society were made up of converts closer to the Hindu lower castes. This was the stage of the formation of the Muslim elite group. During the British period, power relations changed. Now the political game was between two competitors— the Muslim elite and the Hindu elite. The Hindus gained a substantial share in the distribution of power, both economic and political. The Muslims, and particularly the elite among them, could not make much headway because of some inbuilt weaknesses in their social structures. The unequal distribution of power by the British rulers between the two communal groups gave a sharp edge to Muslim communalism. In the course of the power struggle they emerged victorious, achieving the territorial division of the country into India and Pakistan. With the partition of the country, it was assumed that the dead body of communalism would be cremated for all time, and that mourning was done with; it was hoped that free India's efforts for national reconstruction would gain strength and motivation from the new society.

REFERENCES

1. Prabha Dixit, *A Struggle for Power*, New Delhi: Orient Longman, 1974, p. 122.
2. M.N. Srinivas, "The Cohesive Role of Sanskritisation", *Contributions to Indian Sociology*, No. 1, 1957, p. 9.
3. Imtiaz Ahmad, *Caste and Social Stratification Among Muslims in India,* New Delhi: Manohar Publications, 1973, p. 9.
4. Ibid., p. 57.
5. Imtiaz Ahmad, *Family, Kinship and Marriage Among Muslims in India*, New Delhi: Manohar Publications, 1976, pp. 48-49.
6. Ibid., p. 57.
7. Prabha Dixit, op. cit., p. 126.
8. M. Mujeeb, *The Indian Muslims*, London: George Allen and Unwin Ltd., 1967, p. 366.
9. Tara Chand, *History of the Freedom Movement in India*, Vol. II, New Delhi: Publications Division, 1967, p. 10.
10. Ishwari Prasad and S.K. Subedar, *Hindu-Muslim Problem*, Allahabad: Chugh Publications, 1974, p. 115.
11. Ibid., p. 14.
12. K.K. Aziz, *Ameer Ali: His Life and Work*, Lahore: Publishers United, 1968, p. 274.
13. Abdul Majid, Khan, *The Communalism in India: Its Origin and Growth*, Lahore: Paramount Publications, 1944, p. 230.
14. Imtiaz Ahmad, 1973, op. cit., p. 43.
15. Hamid Dalwai, *Muslim Politics in Modern India, 1857-1947*, Bombay: Nachiketa Publications, 1968, p. 134.
16. As quoted in, Asha Sharma, *Socio-Economic Roots of Communalism*, JNU, unpublished M. Phil. Dissertation, 1984.
17. Jyotee Burmah, *Hindu-Muslim Relations: A Study of Historical Background*, Calcutta: Jagnous Sahitya Ghakra, 1947, p. 147.
18. Mushirul Haq, *The Muslim Politics in Modern India*, Meerut: Meenakshi Prakashan, 1970, p. 58.
19. Tara Chand, op. cit., p. 225.
20. K.K. Aziz, *Britain and Muslim India*, London: Heinemann, 1963, p. 142.
21. Op. cit., p. 119.
22. Ishwari Prasad, op. cit., p.172.
23. Said-ud-din Ahmed, *The Commercial Pattern in India*, Lahore: Ashraf Publications, 1947, p. 103.

24. Beni Prasad, *India's Hindu-Muslim Question*, London: George Allen and Unwin Ltd., 1946, p. 205.
25. Tara Chand, "Historical Origins of Communal Problem", *Secular Democracy*, Annual Number, 1974, p. 67.
26. S. Abid Husain, *The Destiny of Indian Muslims*, New York: Asia Publishing House, 1965.
27. Tara Chand, No. 9, op. cit., p. 70.
28. Sir George Schuster and Guy Wint, *India and Democracy*, London: Macmillan, 1941, p. 31.
29. Quoted in Akhtar Usman, *Muslim India*, Lahore: Paramount Publications, 1945, p. 17.
30. K.K. Aziz, 1968, op. cit., p. 48.
31. Rafiq Zakaria, *Rise of Muslims in Indian Politics: An Analysis of Developments from 1885 to 1906*, Bombay: Somaiya Publications, 1970, p. 53.
32. Ibid., p. 57
33. N.G. Barrier (ed.), *Roots of Communal Politics*, Arnold-Heinemann Publishers, 1976, p. 243.
34. Ramji Lal, *Political India (1935-42): Anatomy of Indian Politics,* Delhi: Ajanta Books International, 1986, p. 70.
35. W.W. Hunter, *The Indian Muslims*, Delhi: Indological Book House, 1969.
36. K.K. Aziz, 1968, op. cit., p. 147.
37. Rafiq Zakaria, op. cit., p. 125.
38. S.S. Pirzada (ed.), *Foundations of Pakistan,* Karachi: Metropolitan Publishers, 1969, p. 89.
39. S.A. Lapence, *The Protection of Minorities*, New York: UN, 1967, pp. 125.
40. The Congress, unfortunately, never tried to understand the Muslim character of isolation and aggression, and to the end, continued to dally with the false hope that somehow or the other, some turn of events would remove the communal problem. Bipin Chandra, *Nationalism and Colonialism in Modern India*, Delhi: Orient Longman, 1979, p. 252.
41. S.S. Pirzada (ed.), op. cit., p. 6.
42. K.B. Krishna, *The Problem of Minorities on Communal Representation in India*, London: George Allen and Unwin Ltd., 1939, pp. 90-92.
43. As quoted in Tara Chand, 1967, op. cit., p. 230.
44. Hugh F. Owen, "Negotiating the Lucknow Pact", *Journal of Asian*

Studies, Vol. 31, No. 3, May 1972, pp. 561-587.

45. Mushirul Hasan, *Nationalism and Communal Politics in India, 1885-1930*, New Delhi: Manohar Publications, 1991, p. 72.
46. Quoted in Mohibbul Hasan, "Mahatma Gandhi and Indian Muslims" in S.C. Biswas (ed.), *Gandhi; Theory and Practice: Social Impact and Contemporary Relevance*, Simla: Indian Institute of Advanced Study, 1969, p. 132.
47. P.C. Bamford, *Histories of the Non-Cooperation and Khilafat Movement*, Delhi: K.K. Book Distributor, 1985, p. 138.
48. Ibid., p. 157.
49. Tara Chand, 1967, op. cit., p. 428.
50. Ravinder Kumar, *Essays in Social History of Modern India*, New Delhi: Oxford University Press, 1983, p. 133.
51. S.S. Pirzada, op. cit., p. 575.
52. Prabha Dixit, op. cit., p. 155.
53. K.P. Karunakaran, *Religion and Political Awakening in India*, Meerut: Meenakshi Publication, 1965, pp. 127.
54. Zenab Banu, *Politics of Communalism*, Bombay: Popular Prakashan, 1989, Appendix IV, pp. 180-184.
55. Satish Chandra, "The Roots of Hindu Communalism" in B.N. Pande (ed.), *National Integration*, Bombay: Popular Prakashan, 1970, p. 65
56. Ishwari Prasad and S.K. Subedar, op.cit., p.145.
57. Gangadhar Adhikari, *Indian National Congress and Hindu-Muslim Unity*, Sydney: Current Books, 1943, p. 115.
58. C.H. Philips and M.D. Wainwright (eds.), *The Partition of India: Policies and Perspectives*, London: Allen and Unwin, 1970, p. 145.
59. Ibid., p. 146.
60. R.M. Aggarwal, *Hindu-Muslim Riots: Their Causes and Cure*, Lucknow: International Social Literature Publishing Co., 1943, p. 57.
61. Ibid., p. 125.
62. Sumit Sarkar, *Modern India: 1885-1947*, Bombay: Macmillan India Ltd., 1983, p. 167.
63. Sir William Barton, *India's Fateful Hour*, London: John Murray, 1942, p. 107.
64. As quoted in Tara Chand, *History of the Freedom Movement in India*, Vol. IV, New Delhi, Publications Division, Government of India, 1967, p. 101.
65. Ibid., p. 275.
66. A. Zaidi, "Aspects of the Muslim League's Policy, 1937-1947, in C.M. Philips and M.D. Wainwright (eds.), op. cit., p. 263

67. Ibid., p. 275.
68. K.B. Krishna, op. cit., p. 295.
69. Rafiq Zakaria, op. cit., p. 280.
70. Sandhya Chaudhary, *Gandhi and the Partition of India*, New Delhi: Sterling Publishers, 1984, p. 26.
71. K.K. Aziz, op. cit., 1967, p. 142.
72. Ramji Lal, *Communal Problems in India: A Symposium*, Karnal: Deen Dayal College Publications, 1987, p. 11.
73. S.S. Pirzada, op. cit., p. 337.
74. Zenab Banu, op. cit., p. 28.

3

CHANGING ORIENTATION OF THE STATE

In the last few years we have witnessed an escalation of communalism and consolidation of sentiments around symbols of religious identities and perceptions of threats to these identities. Communal ideologies have gained much wider social acceptance forcing a retreat from even the liberal rhetoric of secularism. But what is particularly striking about the present phase is the role of the State in communalising the political process in overt and covert ways. The reassertion of communalism is promoted not only by communal forces, but also by the institutional regime and the State itself by its indifference and neglect of communalism.

This is something new. Crucial to understanding this new phase of communalism are two aspects: one is the shift in the idiom and discourse of politics; two, the perceptible shift in the orientation of the State. The question is whether the State had fallen prey to forces beyond its control or was it a situation in which institutions and structure in the state apparatus tend to reinforce communalism in the sphere of civil society.

Why did the change take place and what were the political consequences? The orientation has to be seen as part of an overall political shift in the Congress leadership. This involved a move away from the left of centre values of secularism and socialism and towards an ideological discourse, hitherto identified with right wing parties such as the BJP.

Decay of Democratic Institutions

There was a significant change in political discourse. The

shift in orientation was most noticeable in the realm of communalism. Empirical material suggests few insightful explanations for this shift in the orientation of the State. It could best be explained by the detailed study conducted by Myron Weiner[1] twenty-five years ago. It is helpful in describing and explaining broad changes in the governing of India's vast political periphery. The picture that emerges is that of an increasing authority vacuum. The organisational ability of the Congress Party has declined and popular new parties have failed to fill the organisational vacuum. In addition traditional authority patterns in the social structure have been weakened; the capacity of the dominant castes and of other "big men" to influence the political behaviour of those below them in the social hierarchy has diminished. These two trends—the growing democratisation of traditional power relations in the civil society and the failure to create a rational basis of generating new leadership through formal political institutions—are at the heart of the increasing authority vacuum in Indian politics. The vacuum in turn contributes to many of the problems of governability,[2] coalitional instability, the emergence of low quality leaders with damaging rather than progressive appeal, the growing significance of toughs and hoodlums as de facto brokers of local power, ineffective and corrupt local governments and the increasing tendency to resort to violence to state political conflicts.

Weak political institutions have encouraged indisciplined political competition that has politicised all types of social divisions including caste, class and ethnic cleavages. Numerous strategies, including the use of violence, have been used to gain access to the state's resources, thus adding to the growing political chaos.[3]

Organisational weakness in the Congress Party, in conjunction with failure to provide for systematic incorporation of the bottom half of the population into the political process has put a high premium on personal appeal, populism and mobilisation of "primordial" loyalties and strategies for gaining and maintaining power. Those strategies enabled India's ruling party to legitimise its hold on power through democratic means until the end of 1989.

That personalistic and populist ruling style, however, has become a major impediment to the use of state power to solve the nation's problems.[4]

The national political situation in India has thus begun a vicious cycle. It is increasingly difficult to translate personalistic and populist support into the political ability to accomplish policy goals. Policy failures in turn tend to undermine popular support. The strategies for winning power thus come to be even further removed from developmental problems. At the heart of this growing rift between the State's representative and developmental function in Indian politics lies the absence of coherent parties and programmes.[5]

Therefore, power challenges are multiplying and institutional capacity for systematic accommodation of such challenges is not keeping pace. If these trends continue, they are likely to chip away at India's democracy. No problem in contemporary India is likely to prove more serious than the disintegration of its major problem-solving institution, the democratic state.

The analysis of institutional decay has focused attention on the growing disjuncture between weakening institutions and multiplying demands. That manner of conceptualising the problem tends mainly to identify the components of the larger problem. The real explanatory issues have to do with why institutions have weakened. And how and why various groups have been mobilised at the rate and in the manner that they have.

Political variables have played an important role in moulding patterns of political change in India. The State's role in India's political economy has been crucial, the State is not only an agent of political order in India, it is also responsible for promoting socio-economic development. These dual responsibilities have led to a highly interventionist Indian state which organised as a democracy, politics and political competition tends to permeate much of social life. Thus, the nature of India's political structure and the roles played by India's political leaders have been major determinants of political and social change in India.[6]

It is now important to focus sharply on the political structures that have conditioned political change in India and find the answer to the following questions: Why should the Indian State attract so much attention from social groups? What enables a leader to play such a profound role in Indian polity? Why should political mobilisation result not in new organised political initiatives but in chaos?[7] A highly interventionist state tends to politicise all forms of societal cleavages old versus new, social and economic.

In order to understand the decay of India's democratic institutions, it is essential to trace the role of the Congress during 1967. The year 1969 played a significant role in our political system. The Indian political system witnessed serious change with the coming of year 1969. The split in the Congress in 1969 proved fatal for the political future of the Indian State. Factionalism in Congress made it a thought-provoking issue among the power-hungry petty politicians, who at that time had only one question in mind: how to establish themselves as leaders and assure their seat in the power structure. With the split in Congress the new Congress bade farewell to its earlier ideologies.[8]

Since then many developments took place which led to a gradual decline of the role of an institution of infrastructure of popular discussions, of the media and generally of the broad framework of particular and citizen involvement and substitution of it all by the steam roller of winning elections. Since then politics has meant a constant struggle for survival through the number game.

Since 1967, much has changed. Most important, the State's capacity to govern has declined. The surface manifestation of this process has had widespread activism outside the established political channels that has often led to violence, a problem of law and order, corruption and poverty. Below the surface lies the important cause of these political problems, disintegration of India's major political institutions especially the decline of its premier political entity, the Congress party.[9]

Today the Congress Party has lost its hegemony over Indian politics partly as a cause and partly as consequences of its loss of control. Congress has experienced a profound organisational decline. The sprawling party once provided a measure of coherence across the vast and diverse subcontinent.[10]

Age-old hegemonies have crumbled. Ideological doctrines fashioned to perpetuate dominance and control are being widely questioned but equally true is the fact that the age in which we live is also one of growing backlash and crushing repression against the democratic forces.[11] It is also one of growing cooptation of voices of protest and intellectual dissent.While old hegemonies might be crumbling, new ones are being formed and perpetuated. And there is taking place a slow but seductive crystallisation of the doctrines of security stability and unity. These are all being used in pursuit of patterns of governance that are clearly anti-democratic.[12] The very structures that had been conceived for promoting the democratic process and providing liberation from traditional constraints—political parties, representative institutions and judiciary—are becoming vulnerable to the influence of anti-democratic forces and are in any case proving incapable of dealing with them.[13]

Deeper forces of erosion, uncertainty and anomie that are taking hold of the mass mind at a time when the growing vacuum created by the undermining of institutions and the decline in democratic temper is being filled by the specialists in violence, corruption, private arms trade and gang warfare. The sharp decline in the role of the state as a mediator in social conflict and the growing loss of faith in the political process among both the operators of the system and the people at large are products of not just political instability but incipient breakdown of the social order. The result is large-scale social violence, the rise of communal identities and doctrine of exclusion and dispensability, according to which the entire population is looked upon as undesirable and unwanted.

Role of Mrs. Gandhi

Since 1969 is quite prominent, one can even say that the political change which took place in India during 1969-77 and then from 1980 to 1984 is due to Mrs. Indira Gandhi, who had dominated Indian political life. Therefore, to understand the decay of democratic institutions and change in socio-economic policies of India calls for the explanation and critical assessment of Mrs. Gandhi's regime.

Mrs. Indira Gandhi transformed the political system in India, she took India to the process of deinstitutionalising the conduct of public affairs and its substitution by new symbols of managing the public realm and new types of promises and appeals which resulted in a model of nation building and a rhetoric of national unity and national glory and power that split the political community and accentuated the process of polarisation, marginalisation and exclusion of the large mass of the people.[14]

The root of the decay in the national authority structures are to be found in a dilemma that consistently plagued Mrs. Gandhi, keen to maintain her hold on power while facing challenges from the growing demand of power blocks in the polity. Democratic incorporation of such diverse new demands would often have meant a downward transfer of powers. Mrs. Gandhi perceived, not without justification that such moves would weaken the centre and thus both national integrity and the State's capacity to steer economic development.[15] As a consequence, she adopted a recalcitrant stance, instead of accommodating power challenges which might not have been easy in any case; she sought to block their access to power by undermining democratic institutions.[16] Cancellations of elections within the Congress Party, appointment of loyal but weak chief ministers in the states and personalisation of general elections were all part of this ruling strategy.

After the split in the Congress in 1969, Congress (I) went on to improve the political standing by adopting a populist strategy that linked Congress (I) and Mrs. Gandhi directly to the masses. She and her supporters probably did not perceive a need for a strong party organisation in the strategy.[17] She brought about a phenomenal change in the operating culture of politics between 1969 and 1974, after which the process of degeneration and steady erosion set in.[18] This was due to an attempt made by managerial bosses of the Congress Party, the so-called syndicate, to circumscribe her power and threaten her survival in office. To this Indira Gandhi reacted like a dynamo and hitched her personal stakes to a new and unprecedented style and substance of conducting public affairs.[19]

Mrs. Gandhi came forward with a new and catalytic doctrine

and theory that at once caught the imagination of the masses and sought to reverse the political and management model of the Congress system. The doctrine was clear and simple, that in the preoccupation with stability and reconciling opposite tendencies and holding things together, the leadership of the Congress had ignored the condition of the masses and in particular the economic dimension of democracy.[20] Indira Gandhi brought economics to the centre stage of the political agenda, insisted that the task of a democratic state in a poor society was to remove poverty and that there was no escape from adopting a socialist and secular path that would particularly focus on the welfare of the downtrodden, justice and protection for minorities and on eradication of social and economic evils like untouchability and bonded labour and many other forms of gross inequality that still persisted and had in fact grown in spite of the operation of democratic politics and planned economic development.[21]

But the new doctrine implanted by Indira Gandhi in the Indian mass mind, said much had after all been highlighted during the later years. She was criticised for this stand, but she naturally said that the Indian institutional model of reconciling interests and being all things to all people was responsible for growing aspirations and the need was to mobilise the power and underprivileged and discriminated strata into a new coalition of interests that would provide the basis "of the Congress Party's new appeal."[22]

She made full use of the very plurality and differentiations inherent in the Indian social fabric and went for what was later called her winning condition—the rural poor, the Muslims and other religious minorities, the tribals and other ethnic groups and implored them all with the populist rhetoric of *Garibi Hatao* which in turn got closely associated with her own personality and leadership. In the process she opted for symbolic measures of nationalisation and other stock-in-trade of Western-style socialism.[23] She also shifted the institutional base of politics from the party systems, including her own party to the state apparatus from a federal structure to the centre and indeed within the central government from a dispersed ministerial set-up to the Prime

Minister's secretariat, which emerged as the most potent political base of her power, in and around which she inducted some truly imaginative and committed individuals from outside the party.[24]

After the 1971 elections when Indira Gandhi's national popularity was confirmed, many power-hungry politicians switched their allegiance to the Congress.[25] Those who switched, however were not established local politicians. Those joining Congress were newcomers, who were both impatient and wanted promotion in higher level of politics. Her "pro-poor and anti-establishment approach was attractive to this new set but it would not be decisive until it had demonstrated electoral success."[26]

Those who were attracted to the Congress (I) were individuals who felt excluded from the established power structure and wanted power in a hurry. These people had not spent their formative political years participating in the nationalist movement. Rather, they had grown up observing that lucrative careers could be built in a society of scarcity if one had access to the abundant resources of the interventionist state. These were not people who were interested in forming an organisation, their underlying motivations were quite different. Thus, shortcuts to power were sought as a means of simultaneously displacing the dominant groups and gaining access to state resources and Indira Gandhi provided a quick opportunity, the slow laborious task of building party organisation was never carried out.[27]

Mrs. Gandhi went on to improve the political standing of herself and new party primarily by adopting a populist strategy that linked her as a leader directly to the masses. She and her supporters probably did not perceive a need for a strong party organisation in that strategy. Accordingly, Mrs. Gandhi never built the party.[28]

The root of the decay in national authority structure is to be found in a dilemma that consistently plagued Mrs. Gandhi. In order to maintain her hold on power, Mrs. Gandhi sought to ensure her control over the party by appointing those who were loyal to her in the positions of power.[29] Organisational decline within the Congress Party and the inner power disputes, have contributed to the erosion of established patterns of local authority. The institutional patterns of authority have not emerged therefore the institutional vacuum in the periphery in turn helps to explain a number of political trends including coalitional instability and substantial fluctuations in the "political mood". Thus in electoral outcomes, ineffective local governments and the emergence of personal rule, often with ruffians as de facto local leaders.[30]

Mrs. Gandhi's populist rhetoric of course failed to produce results. Not interested in restructuring her party and inducting the mass of the people in its framework and composition through some kind of cadre-building, she relied far too much on the sinews of the state. Congress failed in restructuring the state and its policy apparatus for actually redistributing power, wealth and opportunities ended up creating a top heavy and an increasingly insensitive structure of the state.[31]

Communalisation of the State

When Mrs. Gandhi came to power in 1980, there was tremendous change in her policies. She had shown a shift towards the right. She also gave up her secularism and concern for the minorities and embraced a national chauvinist and communal appeal on the plea of the "nation in danger".[32] She was more pragmatic or by implication less "ideological". Whether labelled "right ward" or pragmatic it is clear that Indira Gandhi's political and policy orientation during that phase as compared with her pre-emergency orientation were different.[33]

The changing political orientation was evident in a number of policy areas. For example communal themes, especially themes of Hindu hegemony that would appeal to India's Hindu heartland, gained currency in Indira's political speeches.[34] After 1980, Mrs. Gandhi sought to build her support in the Hindu heartland and among the business communities by shifting away from the earlier themes of secularism and socialism."[35]

The new political posture had two ingredients : (i) an emphasis on Hindu chauvinism and communalism, that had great appeal in the Hindi heartland, and (ii) a more pragmatic pro-business attitude to accelerate economic growth and to build up her support with industrial and commercial groups.[36]

After 1980 Mrs. Gandhi realised that her political career was at stake. Therefore, she shifted from secular and socialist politics to fascist politics. After the Emergency she had realised that if she wanted to survive in the power structure, she had to shift her vote bank from minorities to majority appeasement, that is to the Hindu North Indian belt, where in the name of Hindu culture she would gain the support of a large voter class.[37]

Mainly there are two points which related to this change in the use of diversity and plural identities.[38] One is the de-ideologisation of politics, and the increasing preoccupation with mere survival in office in which the manipulation of numbers is done on a communal or religious basis. Two, there is a clear backlash against people's movements and mass upsurges. Those in positions of power have seen that a lot of mass unrest growing and organisations at grassroot levels. This situation was expolited by many politicians to promote their vested interests and it often succeeds and even when it does not succeed it still gives rise to radical challenges from the bottom. Very often an attack against a party or a group in the name of national unity is essentially an attack meant to curb popular upsurges which are backing such parties or groups.

The planned destabilisation of the Akali Dal in Punjab or the ouster of the Farooq Abdullah government, through sheer fraud and nothing else, were crucial but striking examples of this. These are examples of patterns that had come up as a result of fairly massive popular upsurge. The other side of the game is backlash against people who would take up the cause of the poor, Dalits, tribals or bonded labour and try to organise them. A lot of this backlash comes from communally-oriented parties including the Congress Party, in which the latter usually succeeds in undermining genuine mass organisation.[39]

Rise in the Sikh, Muslim and Hindu communalism during the 1980s has been the handiwork of the Congress.

We have analysed how the Congress regime since 1967 has eroded the political and social system. Planned erosion of democratic and secular forces has led to the communalisation of state. All the three cases—Punjab episode, Shah Bano case, Ramjanmabhoomi-Babri-Masjid controversy—bear testimony to Congress's role in strengthening communal forces instead of checking them. Communalisation of the State can well be explained through these three episodes.

Punjab Episode

The Punjab conflict is best understood as a political conflict that has been transformed into a fratricidal and ethnic war. The root causes of the turmoil is an intensely emotional matter in India and it attracted considerable controversy.[40] Prior to developing this argument let us look into the origin of Punjab's complex and tragic civil disorder which can be traced in the political conflict between the Congress and Akali Dal.

In many respects Congress, attempted to keep the Akalis out of power after 1980, and the Akalis' repeated attempt to win back Punjab constituted a "normal" political conflict. In its main outline the power struggle involving the centre and regional party was not all that unusual.

There have been certain critical turning points in the politics of modern Punjab that have become permanently embedded into the States' collective political memory. It is important to recall those events briefly. During the linguistic reorganisation of the Indian states in the 1950s the Akali Dal argued for a "Punjabi Suba". The Punjabi-speaking Hindus of Punjab however, fearing Sikh domination, gave their political support to the Hindi speakers of undivided Punjab.[41] Under the influence of the Arya Samaj, a Hindi reform organisation, they declared their language to be Hindi. As a result, the Punjabi-Sikhs and Hindus were one of the few major linguistic groups in India who did not get their own state. The anomaly was corrected in 1969 when the former Punjab was carved into a number of units, including a state for the speakers of the Punjabi language—the contemporary Punjab. The creation of a Punjab of Punjabi speakers, however came about only after prolonged agitations, led mainly by the Sikhs and the Akali Dal.[42] One of the lasting consequences of those early developments was the creation of political distrust among Sikh leaders. Punjabi

Hindus were more likely to ally themselves with the other non-Punjabi Hindus than with the Sikhs.

During the 1950s and early 60s the Akali Dal was controlled by urban Khatri Sikhs typified by Master Tara Singh. Over time however, especially with the rising economic and political significance of the Jat farmers, the leadership passed into the hands of rural landowning groups.[43] Sant Fateh Singh represented this stratum. It was under his leadership, and because of the repeated agitations that he organised in New Delhi that the Centre finally agreed to the creation of a Punjabi Suba in 1966. This victory raised the political popularity of the Akalis within Punjab. In any case, the Congress was by then weakened. Its important first-generation leaders like Pratap Singh Kairon had passed away and left behind a deeply factionalised party. As Congress's overall popularity suffered in India during 1966 and 1967, the Akalis finally emerged victorious. They formed a coalition government in Punjab with the Jan Sangh as junior partner.[44]

The experience of the Akalis in and out of government during 1967-71 had some important political consequences. The fact that the Akalis were in alliance with the Jan Sangh tended to soften both the pro-Sikh communal edge of Akalis and pro-Hindu stances of the Jan Sangh. Thus, the more extreme communal elements among both the Hindus and the Sikhs became available for political mobilization. Congress sought to incorporate both these extreme groups. The more Congress strengthened its alliance with pro-Hindu groups, the more Congress in Punjab came to take on a communal line similar to that of the Jan Sangh.[45]

However, in a peculiar twist that revealed an electoral opportunism runs amok, Congress also encouraged the more extreme Sikh factions within the Akali Dal to break away from their party.[46] The Congress temporarily succeeded in toppling the Akali government in the late 1960s. When that did not last, and the Akalis again formed a ruling coalition, the game of overthrowing the government continued, leading up to the imposition of Presidential rule in 1972.

The series of machinations by Congress must have made it clear to the Akalis that Congress leaders would go to great lengths to secure power in Punjab.[47] The Akalis could mobilise Sikh support around pro-Sikh issues, Congress was just as capable of playing the communal game to achieve political ends. Unfortunately for Punjab, those themselves have continued into the present, contributing to the growing political conflict.

Congress came back to power in 1972. The Sikh hopes of being able to dominate the state of Punjabi speakers proved to be short-lived. The communal arithmetic was seen that the Akalis could control Punjab only if all the Sikhs voted for them. Understanding the issue well, Congress sought to split the Sikh vote; the Akalis in turn tried to unite their power base. During 1973, therefore, with Zail Singh as the state's Chief Minister, Congress sought to portray itself as a champion of Sikh causes and to mobilise Sikhs along religious lines.[48] The Akalis felt compelled to countermobilise. The first version of the Anandpur Sahib resolution, a resolution that sought to consolidate the support of all Sikhs, but especially Jat Sikhs, by demanding greater control for the Sikhs over their own political affairs, was not surprisingly a product of that competitive mobilisational effort by the Akalis.[49]

During the emergency the Akalis vigorously protested Indira's authoritarianism, particularly as a matter of principle, but mainly because the issue offered an opportunity to mobilise the public. Many Akali leaders went to prison. When the embittered Akalis returned to power in 1980, again in alliance with the old Jan Sangh which by then had become the Janta Party, they came down hard on the Punjabi Congressites. Congress fought back. There is evidence to suggest that Congress's support for Bhindranwala originated from that period.[50] Bhindranwala was a popular militant preacher. Zail Singh, who had become the federal home minister, and Sanjay Gandhi apparently concocted the strategy of supporting Bhindranwala in order to weaken the Akalis.[51] It is an open secret that Congress supported Bhindranwala and his candidates in the SGPC elections of 1979. The militants' loss highlighted the Akali moderates' overwhelming dominance in Sikh parties as late as 1979.[52]

While Congress and the Akalis continued to mobilise and conuntermobilise using any means at their disposal, including instigation of religious warfare, Punjabi society had been undergoing important changes.[53] Although there were certain socio-religious changes in society, what finally precipitated conflict were political changes that came after 1980.[54] It was in that year that the Janta Party disintegrated nationally and Congress returned to power with a sizeable majority. It went on to dismiss many of the state governments controlled by the opposition and to call for new state elections.

The Akalis lost power in that national struggle for the third time in a little over a decade. This must have left them with a bitter sense of having repeatedly been wronged by Congress. In the 1980 state elections, however, the Akalis won only 27 per cent of the popular vote. That must have confirmed for Indira Gandhi that she indeed had a right to dismiss an elected government and to call for new elections; in her mind the Akalis had lost popular support.[55] The battle lines were drawn. The centre had the popular support and advantage to consolidate the Congress position and launch a political battle against the Akalis.[56] Congress was successful using Bhindranwala to split the ranks of the Akalis still further between the moderates and the extremists.[57] She enjoyed considerable political advantage by supporting Bhindranwala. Basically she compartmentalised Punjabi society by marginalising the Akalis in 1981-1982.[58]

The Akali Dal, in contrast, had to fight for its life. It had clearly lost considerable popular support, but it continued to possess another set of political resources whose efficacy Congress apparently underestimated.[59] The Akalis could still organise around the issue of Sikh nationalism like no other party in Punjab. The chain of gurudwaras moreover provided a ready organisational network with money, personnel and the proven ability to generate positive support and opinion.[60] The Akali Dal had considerable potential to mobilise the forces of religious nationalism. Both the centre and the Akalis assembled militant forces for political ends. In retrospect, it is clear that over the next several years the military led to civil disorder that took on a political life of its own, increasingly out of the control of both the Akalis and the national government. Whether that simply was not foreseen or was brazenly ignored under the short-term pressure to seize political advantage may never be known.

An early sign of things to come, however, was that Bhindranwala turned against Congress, which had encouraged him to become something of a cult hero.[61] As a result, Bhindranwala began to cultivate his own following. During 1981 and 1982 Bhindranwala increasingly took advantage of his popularity to sever his links with Congress and to enlarge his political base. The repeated failure of the Akalis to wrest power from Congress had left open a political space for those who argued that increased militancy was the only means for protecting Sikh interests. 'Bhindranwala stepped into that space.[62] His appeal combined the themes of religious revivalism and the need for greater political control over the destiny of the Sikhs.[63] Those themes found a ready audience among a significant minority who had come to distrust the manoeuvrings of both Congress and the Akalis. The Akalis thus found themselves being squeezed out of the political process by the militant Sikhs on one side and by Indira Congress on the other.

The failure of the negotiations between the centre and the Akalis during 1982-84 marked an important turning point in the development of the Punjab conflict. It was during those two crucial years that the repeated inability to reach an agreement weakened the hold of the more moderate Sikh leaders over the regional nationalist movement.

This highly condensed account of those complex events makes two things clear: First, the driving force behind the conflict was the power struggle between Congress and the Akali Dal. Both Sikh nationalism and the increasing militancy are better understood as products rather than as sources of the power struggle. Second, because of the failure to achieve a negotiated settlement during 1982-84, the leadership of the movement began to pass out of the hands of those who basically wanted to win elections into the hands of "true believers". The question that remains open however is : why was a negotiated settlement so difficult to achieve?

Most thoughtful observers of Punjab agree that Congress's failure to accommodate Akali demands had less to do with the specifics of the negotiations than with the anticipated political consequences. Clearly, the issue of Chandigarh, allocation of river water and control of the gurudwara were all significant and controversial issues but not important enough to justify the loss of thousands of lives in the anarchy that followed. We now know that during 1982-84, the two sides were close to agreement on two occasions but at the last minute the centre pulled out, without any explanation which may be understood by political analysists as fear of losing power because a settlement would have meant a political victory for the Akalis and would have had adverse electoral consequences for Indira's Congress. That certainty was true within Punjab but possibly elsewhere in north India as well, especially in a state like Haryana which stood to lose Chandigarh and irrigation water in any negotiated settlement.

It is thus clear that Congress's narrow partisan concerns were important causal ingredients in Punjab's tragedy. Many innocent lives would have been saved if Congress (I) had put the longer concern for the public good ahead of concern for Congress's electoral fortunes. In retrospect, therefore, there is little doubt that a more self-assured or more enlightened leader could have put the evolving conflict in Punjab on a different track.

The centre's repeated factors to accommodate the Akali demand reflected its own narrow political considerations, as a national leader's final responsibility for resolving the conflict with Mrs. Gandhi. The failure to do so continued to be a significant debit in her leadership account. Leaders without parties and programmes tend to have narrow political horizons. They also have few institutional constraints on their ambition. The main political actors in Punjab have tended to act on their short-term ambitions, without much regard for the public good. Such an unrestrained power struggle in turn has been a crucial driving force behind the descent towards anarchy.[64]

To conclude this account, the repeated failure of negotiations between the Centre and the Akali leaders continued to swell the ranks of the militants throughout 1983 and 1984. Under militant leadership, many of them began to use gurudwaras as shelters. The prominent leaders eventually made the Golden Temple, the most important Sikh Shrine, their base of operation. Thus the movement of Sikh autonomy come to resemble a theocratic fundamentalist complete with its own "Ayatollahs" and zealous armed forces. Planned murders as well as indiscriminate killings continued to multiply. Hindus were killed by the militants, so as to put pressure on the Congress government. Sikhs were killed so as to minimise dissent within the community. It was this atmosphere that led to the imposition of presidential rule and latter to military assault on the Golden Temple itself. The infamous Operation Blue Star, led to the assassination of Mrs. Indira Gandhi which finally lead to politically directed massacre of a large number of Sikhs all over India, which in turn further compartmentalised the community feeling sharpening the communal hatred among Hindus and Sikhs who once were part of a family.

Muslim Women's Bill 1989/Shah Bano Case

The controversy generated by the Muslim Women's Bill highlighted the role of the government in permitting the growth of a fundamentalist movement and then making use of it in arousing sentiment among the large sections of the people against the so-called appeasement of the minorities.[65]

Why did the government surrender to fundamentalist pressures? The important consideration was the need to stem the anger over the Shah Bano verdict which was losing the Congress its Muslim votes. Following the Congress defeat in the by-elections in Assam, Bijnore, Bishanganj, Bolapur, Kedrappa and Baroda and the belief that everywhere the Muslim vote had tipped the balance in favour of the opposition parties, important Congress leaders advised the Prime Minister against the dangers of a confrontation with the fundamentalists. Syed Shahabuddin's victory in a by-election was a sharp reminder that Congress would suffer electoral reverses in other constituencies as well unless it regained Muslim support.[66]

The decision to bring the Muslim Women's Bill was part of the strategy to reverse the rising tide against the Congress Party's efforts to woo the Muslims. The intervention in favour of the fundamentalists was a desperate bid to regain the Muslim constituency. The government scored progressive opinion raised against the bill and refused to withdraw the bill on the dubious plea that it was framed in deterrence to the wishes of most Muslims. In actual fact, only conservative Muslim groups were consulted and they were passed off as the representative opinion of the community. Within the government, Arif Mohammad Khan raised the banner of revolt. He resigned from the Union Cabinet in protest against the government. His grudge was that the government had given credence to the views of only the conservatives and ignored the secular and progressive opinion in the community.[67]

The political considerations behind the Congress strategy were revealed in the course of the debate on the bill in the Lok Sabha. A.K. Sen, Law Minister defended the introduction of the new legislation by stating that it was the consistent policy of government that in matters pertaining to a community, priority would be given to the leader of the community.[68] This argument assumed that Muslims constituted a self-contained and monolithic community, whose interests were represented by the Muslim MPs and a section of the Ulama.

The most pernicious aspect of the controversy was the attempt by the government to provide the All-India Muslim Personal Law Board-sponsored bill and lament the absence of reformist tendencies against Muslims at the same time. Contrasting the importance of reform amongst Hindus and Muslims, Shiv Shanker, Minister of Commerce, said: "I have the example of various laws with reference to the Hindu community was prepared to accept the law. Whatever we might say here outside the situation is that people (Muslims) are not prepared to accept this".[69] The social logic was unfolded more explicitly by K.C. Pant, Minister of Steel and Mines, "We cannot depend only on the law for reforms. Society has to be ready for reform. The well-springs of that reform have to come from within and then the law that has been aroused by a certain movement, they coincide and then the society moves forward." In Hindu society this process has been going on for decades. It had begun a hundred years ago. As a result of this and the efforts of so many tall leaders of this country the Hindu society has been able to regenerate itself.[70]

These arguments are significant because they expose the contradictions of Congress-style secularism, which sniffed at reform in the name of 'protecting' minority interests. It served an even more important function in the complex structure of Congress politics: the responsibility of the Muslim Women's Bill was transferred to the fundamentalists by arguing that the bill was brought in deference to the wishes of the Muslim community. The massive outcry against the bill forced the Congress to rework its defence by shifting the blame on to the Ministers. Indeed, it would not be an exaggeration to say that on no issue since the imposition of the internal emergency in June 1975 has there been a greater measure of agreement among educated Indians than on this. "It is inconceivable that Rajiv Gandhi and his advisers have not been aware of this reaction", opined Girilal Jain, the influential editor of *The Times of India*. Indeed they were fully aware of the political repercussions of appeasing Muslim fundamentalism.[71] Consequently, the ruling party tried to wash its hands off the bill by taking recourse to the theory that Muslims perceived the Supreme Court verdict as a threat to their religious identity. This theory enabled Congress leaders to delink the party from fundamentalist Muslims by giving the impression that the government was not really in tune with the provisions of the bill but had no choice in the matter because the perception of Muslims was very different.[72]

The subtle shifts in the emphasis could not alter the fact that government was anxious to mollify the fundamentalists. This is most strikingly revealed in the haste with which the legislation was enacted. The opinion of the law ministry was ignored. The legal adviser to the law ministry had categorically stated that the Supreme Court had correctly interpreted the law. The Law Secretary's advice was even more emphatic: The bill to amend the Sections 125 and 127 of the CRPC should be opposed. Assurance given by the Prime Minister of holding wide-ranging consultations were not honoured. Equally, the promise to bring out a background paper on Muslim Personal Law was not fulfilled.[73] And the pleading of the opposition parties not to hasten through the bill was ignored. What is worse the grounds well of the opposition within the ruling party was stifled by the government whip in Parliament.[74]

It is undeniable that the government erred in accepting the demand for a legislation of questionable constitutionality, one which discriminates against Muslim women in relation to other women. Moreover, the bill revealed a major flaw in the pluralist theory of secularism, which functions in practice as multi-theocratic secularism or state protection of all religions and priority of religions.

Ram Janambhoomi-Babri Masjid Controversy

Another indication of the capitulation to communal pressure and the politicians' willingness to play the communal card can be seen from the Ram Janambhoomi controversy. The Ram Janambhoomi Action Committee came into being on October 7, 1984. It launched a 'Tala Kholo' agitation and a Rath Yatra. Indira Gandhi's assassination led to its suspension spearheaded by the VHP. The campaign was revived from twenty-five places on October 23, 1985.[75] In February 1986, the local district judge decided to open the gates on the argument that their locking was no longer necessary for the maintenance of law and order and the protection of the idols. Thus the temple was opened to devotees amidst much fanfare on February 1, 1986.

The opening of the temple was a coup masterminded by the political authorities to appease and conciliate the VHP and Ram Janambhoomi Mukti Samiti who had organised powerful movements to pressurise the Rajiv government to accommodate Hindu sentiments. The strategy employed by these leaders was plainly communal. "How can Rajiv Gandhi ignore the Hindu vote bank which gave him such a massive majority at the polls far exceeding the votes polled by his grandfather?" asked the Hindu leaders.[76] Muslim leaders from the other side of the communal spectrum threatened to boycott the Congress if the Babri Mosque was not restored to Muslims. In fact, the decision to enact the Muslim Women's Bill was a sequel to the pressures mounted by Hindu organisations agitating for the reopening of the Ram Janambhoomi temple.

This was not all. The government played a key role in allowing the shilanyas, processions and campaign to become a vehicle of communalisation and vitiating the political process. Compelled by the sheer interest of garnering votes, the government permitted the shilanyas at a site described by the Allahabad High Court as disputed. What is worse, the government's clarification that the foundation stone was laid at an undisputed site was clearly designed to justify the issue. Besides, the state indulged in dissimulation as it argued that the shilanyas ceremony should pass off peacefully. The issue, however, was not the peaceful nature of the ceremony, but the horrible violence leading up to the ceremony. In Bhagalpur, for instance, hundreds of Muslims were massacred in one of the worst riots after Partition. All this could not have happened without an acceptance of the Ram Shila marriage at the popular level and a high tolerance of its consequences at the official level.[77]

The Ram Shila processions were used by communalists to threaten the wobbling Rajiv Gandhi Government. For them the shilanyas was a power play to demonstrate the strength of the Hindu vote, which the ruling party could ill afford to lose. In spite of the shilanyas, the Congress Party failed to regain the political initiative, after the battering it had received on the use of corruption in high places.

It was a strategy that failed, not because it was communal but because the Congress leaders could not have it both ways, i.e. move from secularism to communalism and vice versa, without creating confusion in the minds of the electorate.

The deliberately engineered communalisation of Punjab, displacement of the National Front in Kashmir, the direct and indirect support and encouragement to Hindu and Muslim fundamentalists as reflected in the aftermath of the Shah Bano judgement and the Ram Janambhoomi-Babri Masjid dispute, the increasing and consistent collapse of the administration and police machinery during communal violence, indicate how the state in India has become communalised and vote-oriented.

All the above three episodes explain the 'Politics of Communalism', that is, how manipulative politics plays the game of divide and rule. It establishes the fact how the state in India has begun to sponsor, encourage and protect communal forces for its own political compulsions and survival, in a blatantly partisan manner.

REFERENCES

1. Myron Weiner, "Congress Resorted: Continuities and Discontinuities in Indian Politics", *Asian Survey*, 12:4, April 1983, pp. 339-355.
2. Atul Kohli, *Democracy and Discontent: India's Growing Crisis of Governability*, Cambridge: Cambridge University Press, 1990, p. 17.
3. Ibid., p. 20.
4. Sudipto Kaviraj, On the Crisis of Political Institutions in India, *Contributions to Indian Sociology,* Vol. 18, No. 2, November 1984, pp. 223-243.
5. Rajni Kothari, *State Against Democracy: In Search of Humane Governance,* Delhi: Ajanta Publications, 1988, p. 96.
6. S. Kaviraj, op. cit., p. 233.
7. Atul Kohli, op. cit., p. 25.
8. Paul R. Brass, *The Politics of India Since Independence,* Cambridge: Cambridge University Press, 1990, p. 88.
9. Atul Kohli, op. cit., p. 21.
10. Ibid., p. 25.
11. Rajni Kothari, "The Crisis of the Moderate System in India and Decline of Democracy" in P. Lyon and J.G. Manor (eds.), *Transfer and Transformation of Political Institutions in the New Commonwealth,* New Hampshire: Leicester University Press, 1983, p. 128.
12. Max Jean Zine, *Strains on Indian Democracy: Reflections on India's Political and Institutional Crisis,* New Delhi: ABC Publishing House, 1988, p. 77.
13. Mushirul Hasan, "Communal and Revivalist Trends in Congress", *Social Scientist,* Vol. 8, No. 7, February 1980, p. 55.
14. Atul Kohli, op. cit., p. 176.
15. Mary C. Canvas, *Indira Gandhi: In the Crucible of Leadership,* Boston: Becon Press, 1979, p. 119.
16. Sudipto Kaviraj, "Indira Gandhi and Indian Politics", *Economic and Political Weekly,* Vol. 21, No. 38/39, September 20-27, 1986, pp. 1697-1708.
17. Lloyd I. Rudolph and Susanne Hoeber Rudolph, "Transformation

of Congress Party: Why 1980 Was Not a Restoration", *Economic and Political Weekly,* Vol. 16, No. 18, May 2, 1981, pp. 811-818.

18. R.P. Sharma, "Indira Gandhi and National Integration", *Journal of Social Sciences,* North-Eastern Hill University, Vol. 5, No.3, July-September 1987, pp. 17-21.
19. Rajni Kothari, op. cit., p. 223.
20. Sujata Patel, "Debacle of Populist Politics", *Economic and Political Weekly,* Vol. 20, No. 16, April 20, 1985, pp. 681-682.
21. Rajni Kothari, *Politics and the People: In Search of a Humane India,* Delhi: Ajanta Publications, 1989, p. 184.
22. Ibid., 184.
23. Atul Kohli, *The State and Poverty in India: The Politics of Reform,* Cambridge: Cambridge University Press, 1987, p. 230.
24. Rajni Kothari, "New Frontier of Politics", *Radical Humanist,* Vol. 54, No.1, April 1990, p. 12.
25. Achin Vanaik, *The Painful Transition: Bourgeois Democracy in India,* London and New York: Verso Books, 1990, p. 186.
26. Kohli, op. cit., p. 55.
27. O.P. Grewal and K.L. Tuteja, "Communalism and Fundamentalism: A Dangerous Form of Anti-Democratic Politics", *Economic and Political Weekly,* Vol. 25, No. 47, November 24, 1990, pp. 2592-2593.
28. Pradeep Nayar, "Congress Party and Political Stability", *Mainstream,* Vol. 29, No. 29, May 11, 1991, pp. 14-16.
29. Henry C. Hart (ed.), *Indira Gandhi's India: A Political System Reappraised,* Boulder, CO: Westview Press, 1976, p. 217.
30. Eddle Girdner, "Social Ferment in India", *Bulletin of Concerned Asian Scholars,* Vol. 19, No. 3, July-August 1987, p. 57.
31. Henry C. Hart (ed.), op. cit., p. 238.
32. Ibid., p. 135.
33. James G Manor, op. cit., p. 80.
34. Atul Kohli, "Politics of Economic Liberalisation in India", *World Development,* Vol. 17, Issue No. 3, 1989, pp. 305-328.
35. Javed Abbass, "Political Articulation of Mass Consciousness in Present-day India", in Zoya Hasan et. al. (ed.), *State, Political Process and Identity: Reflections on Modern India,* New Delhi: Sage, 1989, p. 236.
36. Harbans Mukhia, "Communalism and Indian Polity", in Bidyut Chakrabarty (ed.), *Secularism and Indian Polity,* New Delhi: Segment Book Distributors, 1990, p. 87.

37. Zoya Hasan, "Changing Orientation of the State and the Emergence of Majoritarianism in the 1980s, *Social Scientist,* Vol. 18, No. 8/9, August-September, 1990, pp. 27-37.
38. Rajni Kothari, "The Great Divide", *Illustrated Weekly,* September, 1985, p. 11.
39. Harbans Mukhia, op. cit., p. 92.
40. Sucha Singh Gill and, K.C. Singhal, "The Punjab Problem: Its Historical Roots", *Economic and Political Weekly,* Vol. 19, No. 14, April 7, 1984, p. 604.
41. Ibid., p. 605.
42. Ibid.
43. Mark Tully and Satish Jacob, *Amritsar; Mrs. Gandhi's Last Battle,* London: Jonathan Cape, 1985, p. 60.
44. Dalip Singh, *Dynamics of Punjab Politics,* New Delhi: Macmillan, 1981, p.104.
45. Ibid., p. 220.
46. Pritam Singh, "Lessons of Panchayat at Elections", *Economic and Political Weekly,* Vol. 18, No. 43, October 22, 1983, pp. 1822-1823.
47. Khushwant Singh, "Genesis of Hindu-Sikh Divide", in Amarjit Kaur et. al. (ed.), *The Punjab Story,* New Delhi: Roli Books, 1984, p. 127.
48. Pritam Singh, "Growing Separatist Trend", *Economic and Political Weekly,* Vol. 19, No. 5, February 4, 1984, pp. 195-196.
49. Rajiv A. Kapur, *Sikh Separatism: The Politics of Faith,* London: Allen and Unwin, 1986, p. 147.
50. Pritam Singh, 1984, op. cit., p. 196.
51. A.S. Narang, *Storm Over the Sutlej: The Akali Politics,* New Delhi: Gitanjali, 1983, p. 135.
52. Dalip Singh, op. cit., p. 242.
53. Khushwant Singh, *A History of the Sikhs,* Vol. 2, New Delhi: Oxford University Press, 1966.
54. Ibid., p. 123.
55. Gopal Singh, "Socio-Economic Bases of the Punjab Crisis", *Economic and Political Weekly,* Vol. 19, No. 1, January 7, 1984, p. 42.
56. Robin Jaffrey, *What's Happening to India? Punjab, Ethnic Conflict and the Test for Federalism,* Hong Kong: Macmillan, 1986, p. 5.
57. D.L. Sheth and A.S. Narang, "The Electoral Angle", in Amrik Singh (ed.), *Punjab in Indian Politics: Issues and Trends,* Delhi: Ajanta Publications, 1985, p. 126.
58. Ibid., p. 127.

59. Gurharpal Singh, "Understanding the Punjab Problem", *Asian Survey,* Vol. 27, No. 12, December 1987, pp. 1268-77.
60. Khushwant Singh, op. cit., p. 134.
61. Harish K. Puri, "The Akali Agitation: An Analysis of Socio-Economic Basis of Protest", *Economic and Political Weekly,* Vol. 18, No. 4, January 22, 1983. p. 115.
62. Gopal Singh, op. cit., p. 46.
63. Paul R. Brass, op. cit., 1990, p. 169.
64. Mohinder Singh, *The Akali Movement,* New Delhi: Macmillan, 1978, p. 230.
65. Zoya Hasan, "Minority Identity, Muslim Women's Bill Campaign and the Political Process", *Economic and Political Weekly,* Vol. 24, No. 1, January 7, 1989, pp. 44-50.
66. Ibid., p. 48.
67. Ibid., p. 46.
68. *The Times of India,* March 4, 1986.
69. A.R. Saiyed, "Secularism in Retreat: The Communal Secular Paradox in India", in Bidyut Chakrabarty (ed.), *Secularism and Indian Polity,* New Delhi: Segment Book Distributors, 1989, p. 149.
70. Zoya Hasan, "Changing Orientation of the State and the Emergence of Majoritarianism in the 1980s", *Social Scientist,* Vol. 18, No. 8/9, (August-September 1990), pp. 27-37.
71. Sumit Gangwal, "Communalism and Political Process", *Political Science Review,* Vol. 27, No. 1-4, January- December, 1988, p. 180.
72. A.G. Noorani, "BJP's Assault on Minorityism: Lesson from Britain", *Economic and Political Weekly,* Vol. 25, No. 33, August 18, 1990, p. 1809.
73. *The Statesman,* April 20, 1986.
74. *The Times of India,* July 16, 1990.
75. R.K. Hazari, "Communalism: Perception and Counter Perceptions", *Mainstream,* Vol. 24, No. 48, August 2, 1986, pp. 7-9.
76. Ashish Banerjee, "A Note on Recent Trend in Communal Politics in India", in Bidyut Chakrabarty (ed.), op. cit., 1990, p. 220.
77. C.P. Bhambri, "State and Communalism in India", in K.N. Panikkar (ed.), *Communalism in India; History, Politics and Culture,* Delhi: Manohar Publications, 1991, p. 130.

4

COMMUNAL VIOLENCE AND THE STATE

We are entering an extremely dangerous phase to find that communalism has made serious inroads into the state apparatuses, many of the officials of government have openly or secretly compromised with or even supported communal forces and sometimes themselves practised communalism. The law and order machinery has to get rid of communal elements. It has to remain ever vigilant to extinguish the communal spark before it sets an area or town on fire.

We need a state machinery which is efficient and impartial enough to suppress communal riots and ensure safety of all Indian citizens. And we need at the helm of affairs men and women who are genuinely above communal prejudice. It is a tragedy that we have fewer and fewer of such men and women amongst us today.

Contrary to the general impression, religion is not the root cause of the Hindu-Muslim conflict: it is rather a powerful instrument in the hands of those interests which seek to play their game through it. Competition for jobs, land, economic gain or political power is the root cause for communal clashes. The communalisation of Indian politics and the creation of communal "Vote Banks" have an important bearing on communal conflicts in our society. Moreover, in a backward and communally divided society, the elites of the respective communities, taking advantage of economic disparities, are able to exploit religious sentiments among the lower economic class. The thrust of the argument is to analyse the role of the state in controlling, combating and manipulating communal violence. Since 1984 communal violence has become part of the system. In this chapter an attempt has been made to study that state which was considered the custodian of our welfare but has turned into a repressive institution.

Communal violence is a complex social phenomenon with vast dimensions. Decisive explanations and various perceptions have been propounded to analyse communal violence. All these perceptions are valuable yet none is conclusive in itself. However, the fact remains that the phenomenon of communal strife has alarmingly increased as indicated by the index of communal riots in post-Independence India. The growth appears to be parallel at times larger in size than the socio-economic development of Indian society.

The inter-religious tensions and strikes have increased despite the fact, as observed by Wilcox, that all groups in India crucial to success of the inherited participant economic and political culture entrepreneurs, labour leaders, bankers, judges and barristers, bureaucrats, soldiers, legislators and party bosses at all levels of society—national, state and local have grown in strength, size and confidence in India.[1] Communalism is an ideology which advocates that the followers of a religion have common interest and followers of another religion have different interests. It is an ideology which preaches hatred against the followers of other religions or religious communities.

While communalism is an ideology, "communal violence is a manifestation of this ideology. A communal conflict or an act of communal terrorism with the suddenness of its outbreak and its toll of hundreds and thousands dead, it is an episodic consequence of the spread of communal ideology." It is a concrete manifestation and product of prior communalisation of the people. Communal ideology can prevail without violence but violence cannot exist without communal ideology.[2]

Communalism leading to inter-religious conflicts and violence is endemic to the Indian plural society. Such conflicts have been at times spontaneous outbursts and at times, the result of well comprehended and carefully designed manoeuvres on the part of a particular religious group against another. Communal violence resulting in rioting between Muslims being a dominant minority religious group and Hindus a preponderant majority has been a perennial problem of the Indian society.

Historically, inter-religious conflicts resulting in violence have been few and far between in India. The first inter-religious clash which can be authenticated by records took place in 1730 in Ahmedabad in the modern Indian state of Gujarat.[3] However, the occurrence of communal violence as a regular social phenomenon started from 1922 onwards. Thus, during 1922–27, in a period of the first five years, 450 people died and 5000 were injured in the intermittent communal violence in India.[4] However, the manner in which politics in India was pursued after 1920 on communal lines creating a divide between these two communities provided a raison d'etre for such conflicts. This process culminated in 1947 with the division of India, when millions of people got massacred in the communal frenzy unleashed by the partition of the country.

In the post-Partition era, for a few years it appeared as if India had overcome the spell of inter-religious strife and conflict. After the assassination of Mahatma Gandhi, it was felt and believed that India would usher in an era of Ahmisa (non-violence). However, this peace proved to be illusory and the silence was broken in 1951 by the Cooch Bihar riots and communal violence in West Bengal. The frequency of these incidents increased from 1954 and thereafter communal violence started taking place in a patterned manner.

A great deal of work has been done to study and analyse the phenomenon of inter-religious conflict. The scholars who undertook the case studies of many communal conflicts have attempted to analyse and provide some plausible explanations for the prevalence of this phenomenon.[6] Occasionally, the government also appointed commissions of inquiry to look into the factors of such conflicts and suggest remedies to control them.[7]

Some noteworthy explanations which flow out of these case studies and reports are as follows:

1. The conflicts of such nature may be traced to economic factors which involve the acquiring of economic prosperity.

The commercial competition between the groups belonging to divergent religions bring about such conflicts. For instance, in Bhiwandi, the handloom business, and in case of Meerut and Moradabad, the brass-ware business. The reports have tried to establish that competition among the members belonging to diverse religious groups to monopolise a particular commercial activity has resulted in such conflicts and violence. Hence, it is concluded that the more the competition grows, the greater the possibility of conflicts of this nature in society.[8]

2. Electoral politics has been determining the objectives and directions of communal violence by mobilising people on caste/communal lines. The riots in Hyderabad (Andhra Pradesh), Jalgaon, Aurangabad and Pune (Maharashtra) are indicated as instances of this.[9]
3. The conflicts and violence on communal lines are accentuated by the nexus of traders indulging in illicit trade practices or underworld goons and government officials and businessmen. In the Baroda riots, a nexus between bootleggers and politicians and in Ranchi, a nexus between goons and businessmen was established.[10]
4. The present developmental process and the changing socio-economic milieu of India having changed the caste dynamics and accorded new privileges to the castes, made them easy targets of mobilisation on religious grounds. The Bihar Sharif riots are indicated as an instance of this.[11]
5. Inter-religious conflicts are used by the government to divert the attention of the population from genuine problems. The anti-reservation agitation (against the Scheduled Castes and other Backward Classes reservation, professional colleges and government jobs) in Ahmedabad in 1985 is cited as an example. This agitation, which was essentially an intra-communal conflict, was conveniently turned into an inter-religious conflict.[12]

The theories on communal violence and inter-religious conflicts formulated as a consequence of the case studies and on the basis of the reports of the commissions of inquiry have led to a great deal of debate and discussion. The focal point of discussion has been whether the economic and political factors are responsible for communalism and inter-religious conflicts manifesting themselves in communal violence.

Moin Shakir maintains that electoral politics, that is, nominations of candidates, campaigning, communal representation, etc. accentuated the process of communalism in every state of India.[13] He, however, relates the phenomenon of the conflict to the exploitative forces in Indian society. According to Shakir, "Communalism practised by both the majority community or the minority communities is in consonance with the interests of ruling class/classes. Its presupposition of well-knit and homogeneous communities, its association of Hindu, Muslim, Sikh or Christian interests, and its reliance on religion for mobilising the people comes in the way of changing the political status quo an property relations".[14] Shakir concludes his thesis with the remark that the fight against communalism is a part of the fight for consistent democracy and of class struggle which implies the completion of anti-feudal and anti-bourgeois revolution.[15] In fact, there are a number of scholars and analysts who subscribe to this interpretation of communal conflicts in India.

There is some relevance in the argument that communalism and inter-religious conflicts have become a stumbling block in the way of consolidation of people on the basis of class. It is equally true that such conflicts are preventing the deprived classes from launching a common struggle against the exploitative and discriminative structures of society. But it is doubtful whether the phenomenon of inter-religious conflict can be directly ascribed to a particular class of society. Instances are not lacking when the unity of a group as a class proved to be illusory, and groups did get divided on communal and religious lines during a strife.[16] In the same manner, the grassroots movements to organise the workers on the basis of their common interests proved to be weak to stem the onslaught of communal violence.[17] That is why analysts have not accepted the economic and political factors to be "necessary and sufficient conditions for inter-religious conflict and violence."[18] A.R. Saiyed maintains that as a matter of fact, interested individuals and groups often seize the opportunity to derive economic gains after the communal riots have begun.[19] This is not the same as economic interests causing riots. Yet numerous ex-post facto analyses tend to postulate consequent conditions as antecedents. Moreover, universal referents are also lacking in support of such formulations. Ratna Naidu, a sociologist who has investigated a number of communal riots and analyzed the phenomenon of inter-religious strife, also rejects the thesis of "many a communal tension leading to a riot having economic variable as a direct explanation."

Anatomy of Hindu-Muslim Riots

If we were merely to take a surface view of the bare facts of any riot, it would appear that the riot was caused by an incident so insignificant that we would be amazed at how such a trifling matter could have led to so much arson, looting and murder. It however, does not require deep thinking to know that this incident was not the real cause of the riot but was merely the result of something else which concretely expressed itself in the riot. The basic cause of all communal disturbances is the communal atmosphere pervading the country and the communal tension built up between the two communities. The communal atmosphere provides a ready-tilled soil for communal-minded people to sow seeds of communal hatred and nurture them till the bitter harvest of a communal riot is reaped.

Communal philosophy and ideas constantly propagated in communal papers and journals and from communal platforms have so poisoned the minds of the ignorant sections of the two communities and even of certain sections of the educated and literate class that every action of a member of the opposite community is looked upon with distrust and suspicion and the most uncharitable construction placed upon it. In some cases, even officials whose duty is to hold the balance evenly between the two communities are not found free of the taint.[20]

Communal violence, like wars is also born in the minds of people. The socio-economic, religious and political causes only aggravate the disease of communal violence. It is therefore, imperative that efforts are made not only to secularise, but government and the administrative machinery, particularly police personnel as well as the masses who must learn not only to tolerate each other but also to respect human life and dignity and respect law, with reference to the rights and duties of all citizens, irrespective of caste, creed and community.

The mutual dislike and distrust prevailing between an average Hindu and an average Muslim in India has been aptly illustrated by Mr. A.D. Gorwala, who expresses the opinion as follows: "To the Hindu, the Indian Muslim is a renegade or the son, grandson or great grandson of fourth degree of a renegade. He is either himself or through his ancestors, a man who has been false to the original faith in which he or they are born."

"To the Muslims, the Hindu is a crafty, low person, born only to be ruled over and because of his numbers always trying to filch away others' rights. There is in the Hindu neither frankness nor generosity. He is a mean, calculating, sawing type full of cunning but with no breadth of mind or spirit. Deception is his forte and fair is to him a quality to ridicule and they (Hindu) try to establish superiority over us, the rightful rulers of the land, who held it by force of arms for hundreds of years and treated them as subjects, not at all badly."[21]

It is obvious that the mutual dislike and distrust between the two major communities living in India, as indicated above are mainly due to ignorance and prejudice, which must be eradicated through liberal and secular education.

All the available data shows that political power in India has been the monopoly of the rich and the neo-rich. At the lower level of Indian politics what one notices is the emergence of the neo rich as a political force in a big way. The neo-rich elements control the centres of politics and economics. The neo-rich category by its very definition, carries some element of lumpishness and is characterised by ruthlessness and by the absence of sophistication. It is devoid of all values. This development strengthened the bourgeois character of Indian democracy. It has a vested interest in communal and caste violence as a means of maintaining its position in the system by dividing the people and for diverting their attention from the real problems.[22]

The ruling class in India has developed a strategy to tackle the problem of social violence, a strategy which really originated with the colonial rulers. The demands of the elite of all communities are supported, but the demands of the masses of the communities are suppressed. Violence which does not distrust the status quo is handled in a cursory manner. In cases of mob anger and violence, not only the 'haves' but also the 'government' acts as assassinator. Coupled with this is the fact that Hindu extremists and chauvinist groups are making inroads into rural areas. This is creating a situation in which killings are so planned that no opportunity is available to the victims for resistance or retaliation.[23]

The role of politics in communal violence can be understood in a number of ways. Since economic growth is taking place at a very slow rate the politicians can indulge only in politics of distribution and not of production. Politics being the art of the possible, the politicians find it more paying in terms of votes to appeal in the name of caste, religion and language. Thus local politics often assumes the character of a zero-sum game with built-in potential for social conflict. At the same time, since in a mixed constituency legislators have to depend on the vote of both the communities, the Muslim legislation belonging to all-India parties are often constrained to eschew the more militant form of protest, as far as Muslim causes are concerned and are obliged to work behind the screen.[24]

In most cases, the riots are politically motivated. Also, in almost all riots, the role of rumours in rousing communal passions is quite prominent. It is reported that the knives used by rioters were used in a particular manner, suggesting that the users are trained to handle the knife. Of late, the participants in the riot have begun using lethal weapons and bombs.[25]

Riots are pre-planned and politically-oriented, preceded by almost identical incidents which rouse religious passions followed by the desired similar results conducive to the growth of anti-secular politics.[26] Rajni Kothari, while analysing the phenomenon of inter-religious conflict in modern India, relates it to the electoral politics of the post-Independence era. He provides a provocative explanation "since then politics has meant a constant struggle of survival. Survival through the number game."[27] Once this happened, the notion of pluralism in democracy got perverted into communalism by emphasising the numerical power of majorities versus minorities. In this sense those who argue that communalism is a direct child of secular politics are right. Thus, viewed from this perspective, the phenomenon of inter-religious conflict appears to be essentially related to the struggle for power, political power and generation of inter-religious conflicts in a multi religious society becomes an imperative on the part of those who are involved in the struggle for power. The success of the vanquisher would depend on how deep are the cleavages one succeeds in making in society among the varied religious groups.[28]

The communal trends were set in motion in a patterned form in Indian society after the potential of dissociative and divisive processes generated through inter-religious conflict was fully realised. These trends were generated, first at the local levels, then at the regional levels and finally at the national level. The inputs to sharpen the conflicts also increased in size and dimension over a period of time. Thus, the phenomenon of conflict has moved from one orbit to another, till it acquired a shape and form which ceased to be communalism and which used to be described as 'moderate' as well as essential to a multi-religious society. Rajni Kothari wonders "for we are witness to a new version of communalism".[29]

A new phase it may be but it is more than just a phase. It is communalism, that does not even wear the same face any more. Having traversed varied phases of its history the phenomenon entered a new phase of competitive communalism. In an attempt to outmanoeuvre each other, the groups started acquiring visible militant postures, at times challenging the authority of the state.[30] And evidence is not lacking where even the instruments of state got involved in inter-religious strife and clashes. With more and more consolidation of their ranks, these groups realised the need to play a supplementary and complementary role to each other and this they did initially overtly and later on quite covertly.

Today as we trace ourselves out of 1984, India's power centre has collapsed, the spectre of disunity haunts us. The authorities in power are unable to administer, without increasing resort to para military and military force. Our large and creative minorities are fast losing faith in the system while the people at large feel rudderless and are driven by forces beyond their control.[31] This new face of communalism has two aspects. First, it is not an observation but something that is part of the system. Second, this is not so in any passive way, where the "system" has fallen prey to forces beyond its control. Rather, it is a direct outcome of its inherent logic and one in which its key actors play a role.[32]

What is relatively marked about the present phase is that the ruling party and state itself are playing a direct role in communalism of the society. The developments in Bombay, Bhiwandi, Ahmedabad, Delhi, Bokaro and Kanpur, Bhagalpur, Surat and more recently in Gujarat have highlighted the role of the government and ruling party in spreading terrorism, inciting and even engineering communal violence permitting the growth of chaos and vandalism and then making use of its all-arousing chauvinistic sentiments among large sections of the people. Still more recently, the 'riots' in Gujarat, Delhi, Meerut, Bhagalpur, Surat have brought out the role of gangster politicians.[33]

The State's involvement in communal violence can be traced since 1984 first during the Meerut riots and after that what happened in December 1984 proves that the involvement of the state machinery was not purely through negative acts of omission by being unavailable to the victims, but through acts of participation. Witness has testified to the participation of police personnel not only in disarming Sikhs but in promoting and initiating actual acts of looting and rape.[34]

The PUCL Report cites an evidence, when after the destruction and murders people went to complain and file FIRs. The police in many cases refused to record their complaints according to information gathered from the Hindu neighbours of the victims.[35]

In Kotla Mubarakpur, a domestic worker told the PUCL team members that the police had encouraged the looting. Later they were reported to have said to the looters, "We gave you 36 hours. Had we given the Sikhs that amount of time, they would have killed every Hindu."[36]

Systematic movement of truckloads of rioters and kerosene came from Harayana into Delhi. It was worth noting that such a movement went unnoticed given the automatic alert which sealed Delhi within hours of the assassination. All these activities, we realised were the systematic rituals of a terrorist state.[37]

The evidence available is awesome. Consider first the sheer scale of logistics that the recent genocide involved as an information system. It demanded the prompt identification of all Sikh households in each locality. Such immediate identification could not have been done without the concurrence of ration shop and kerosene depot owners and occasionally by headmasters who used school registers for identification. Beyond the logistics of information lies the logistics of the supply area. Kerosene was distributed widely in handcarts. In South Delhi, Delhi Transport (DTC) buses were used by marauding gangs.[38]

The violence of the Delhi riots was all too often premeditated. In an area of Delhi University, pits were dug and labelled "Sardar Ghat" in anticipation. Even as regards the style of violence, the systematic burning of human beings was something new. Doctors attest to the difficulty of burning a human body and the presence of phosphorus comes as a frightening act of premeditation.[39]

All this leads us to conclude that what we had witnessed in 1984 was not the spontaneous upsurge of communal violence but the development over time of a new technology of oppression under the aegis of the state. As typologists of violence, we realised that we were confronting not an act of a small group of terrorists as in Punjab or a communal riot as in Hyderabad or Jamshedpur. What we witnessed was calculated organised terror by the state against the members of a community. It is this specific context that the sociology of Delhi city in 1984 provides an evidence to the arrival of an anti-people state.[40] Riots were assuming the character of "cleaning up operations" by the state since November 1984.

Bhagalpur Riots 1989

It has become common in recent writings to describe one instance of strife after another as "perhaps the worst since 1947". Such has been the magnitude and brutality of sectarian violence in the 1980s.[41] Bhagalpur, 1989, was one of these devastating outbreaks. This round of violence in Bhagalpur began in the last week of October 1989. Arson, loot and murder spread from the city to the surrounding countryside and raged practically unchecked for several days. The situation was then brought under some sort of control by military and paramilitary forces; but an atmosphere of fear and terror remained for months afterwards.

Given the scale of the riot and the infamous role of the local administration in encouraging the attacks and suppressing evidence, it is impossible to establish the 'facts' of the occurrence—what traditional historians like to call the 'nuts and bolts' of the story.[42] Possibly as many as 1000 people were killed in the course of the violence, most of them Muslims but estimates of the casualities still vary enormously.[43] During the first days of the 'riots', trains were stopped repeatedly at different places in Bhagalpur and its neighbouring districts and from several of these Muslim travellers were dragged out and lynched but no one can say for certain how many were killed in this way—not even disturbed Hindu travellers who happened to be caught on one of these trains and saw people being pulled out and killed. In the major attacks, in the rural areas as well as in the city, neither old people nor infants, neither women nor children were spared. There is a widespread feeling that women were abducted and raped on a large scale, but none of the surviving victims will talk about rape. The five specific cases recorded by the PUDR team that conducted investigations in Bhagalpur in January 1989 were incidents which the Muslim women informants had themselves heard about.

What is beyond question is that the extent and ferocity of the attacks was quite unprecedented, even for a district which has seen much sectarian strife before, including riots in 1946. At the worst stage of the violence in October-November 1989, some 40,000 people were forced to leave their homes and live in makeshift relief camps. Destruction and looting of property occurred on a massive scale for several weeks. The fears generated among the heavily outnumbered Muslims were such that a great many were unwilling to return to their homes. Even three months after the initial outbreak of violence, an estimated 10,000 were still in 'relief camps' towards the end of January 1990, apart from those who had moved in with relatives or friends in safer places in or outside Bhagalpur district.[44]

At this time many Muslims were pressing for the permanent retention of military or para-military forces in the vicinity of their villages or wards (mohallas), as the only trust worthy means for their protection, and some were demanding that they be given arms by the government for the same purpose. The air was still thick with rumours and isolated attacks and looting continued to occur. One such incident was reported as late as March 1990.[45]

What is of concern is that much of the official record on the basis of which historians and social scientists gather facts is reported missing. This reliable source which is considered authentic has been largely destroyed for the first few days of riots which were most critical. A *Sunday Mail* report of February 19, 1990[46] made after a fortnight-long investigation into the Bhagalpur carnage and its aftermath sums up the situation in this regard.

> Crucial records of the period, especially those from the tables of the then district magistrate (DM) and superintendent of Police(SP) are missing. Even the joint report of the DM and the SP on the first incident at Tatarpur Chowk in Bhagalpur city on October 24 that had lit the fuse is among the papers not traceable.[47]

This kind of destruction or removal of records is of course not unprecedented, the British practised it on a large scale in India after 1937 and no doubt there have been many other instances since Independence. What is less frequently observed however, is the destruction entailed in the systematic construction of evidence on all sides, official and unofficial. When an event of this kind occurs, violence produces the necessity of evidence gathering of uncovering hidden processes and contradictions that we might normally prefer to ignore, but violence also wipes out 'evidence' and even to a large extent, the possibility of collecting it in a manner and form that is deemed acceptable by today's social science.[48] The thrust of the above statement made by Gyanendra Pandey is that history is based on archives, records or whatever material is available from an official source is considered to be a reliable source, but if evidences are destroyed and negligent handling of materials by the state machinery are an ample evidence in itself to prove the fact that the state is party to such social tensions.

We have to rely on PUDR and other such voluntary organisations for the inside information which led to these riots. The incidence worth noting regarding the Bhagalpur riots is that a documentary film on the Bhagalpur riots was prepared by Nalini Singh, which was made after thorough investigations and research, but the point to be emphasised here is that this documentary was not allowed to be telecast on Doordarshan "in as it is form". It was cleared for the national network only after going through censorship, where necessary cuts were made. Still, after going through censorship that documentary was a bold step by Nalini Singh, in which the state emerged as the prime culprit.

During the Bhagalpur riots some facts have come to light. Many observers have pointed to the new heights reached by Hindu military and propaganda over the last two years.[49] This has been orchestrated most visibly by the Vishwa Hindu Parishad (VHP) and plainly had much to do with the increased frequency and scale of Hindu-Muslim strife in the 1980s. The point that is perhaps not sufficiently stressed however is that the violent slogans and demands of organisations like VHP, and the riots they have sparked off do not poison the minds of the people only for a moment. On the contrary, given our history, the resources available to secular and communal forces in the country, the opportunism of most of our major political parties, and the continued and repeated outbreak of sectarian violence, the most outrageous suggestions about the evil dangerous, threatening character of the other community (or communities)[50] come to be widely accepted and to become part of popular dogma.

Nothing but this acceptance can explain the kinds of atrocities perpetrated in recent instances of sectarian strife, the call to leave not a single Muslim, man, women or child alive, which was acted upon in several places in Bhagalpur—the massacre of all eighteen Muslim passengers travelling in a tempo-taxi along with a Hindu taxi driver, when they were stopped on a major country road two and a half weeks after the cessation of general rioting and their burial in a field which was then planted over with garlic, the chopping of the breasts of women, the spearing of infants and children, the spears with the victims impaled on them being then twirled around in the air to the accompaniment of laughter and shouts of triumph.[51]

What lies behind this insane and incredible brutality is the belief that the victims are real or potential monsters who have done all this and worse to us or will do so, if given half a chance. In many cases, the alleged atrocities for which these actions are supposed to be just recompense are believed to have occurred 'yesterday' or the other day or two in a neighbouring district or further away in Bhagalpur. The rumour that set off the major Hindu attacks in the countryside, was that all the Hindu students living in Muslim owned boarding houses, in a part of the city near the university, had been massacred on the first two days of the riots.[52] In other instances revenge appears to be sought for what they have done to us generally in the past. Since the 1980s there has been an organised campaign launched by the VHP, RSS for the communalisation of society. This statement can be ascertained by the following facts and statements made by the VHP to which the state has intentionally turned a deaf ear.

The VHP propagates that all Muslims in India are Pakistanis, because whenever there is a cricket match between India and Pakistan, they (Muslims) side with Pakistan. Following from this argument that the local Muslims are out to create another Pakistan in one place after another Bhagalpur, Moradabad, Meenakshipuram (Tamil Nadu). By this juncture we are into that realm where "Muslims" are represented as being inherently turbulent, fanatical, violent.[53]

Hindu historians and propagandists claim that aggression, conversion, unbounded sexuality, are the themes that make up the history of the spread of Islam "wherever Muslim communities exist there will inevitably be a dance of annihilation in the name of Islam." It is the religious duty of every Muslim to "kidnap and force into their own religion, non-Muslim women." Several pamphlets and leaflets distributed by militant Hindu organisations in places where strife has lately occurred set the picture of a Hindu husband and wife with two children–*"Ham do, Hamaare do"* (We Two Our Two) by the side of a Muslim family man with four wives and numerous children accompanied by the self-explanatory slogan–"*Ham Paanch, Hamaare Pacchis*" (We Five, Our twenty-five).[54] Thus, a whole new "common sense" develops relating to the marital and sexual practices of the Muslims referring only to Muslim men, to their perverse character and the violent temperament.[55]

It will perhaps suffice to illustrate the tenor of recent Hindu propaganda and beliefs about the Muslims by reproducing the contents of one of the leaflets distributed in Bhagalpur sometime between the last quarter of 1989 and January 1990 entitled 'Hindu Brother Consider and Be Warned'.[56] The leaflet asks:

(a) Is it not true that the Muslim population is increasing while that of the Hindus is decreasing?

(b) Is it not true that the Muslims are fully organised (prepared) while the Hindus are fully disorganised (scattered)?

(c) Is it not true that the Muslims have an endless supply of weapons, while the Hindus are completely unarmed?

(d) Is it not true that the Congress has been elected to power for the last 40 years were 30 per cent of the vote and in other words that the day the Muslims become 30 per cent of the population, they will gain power?

(e) Is it not true that the Muslims will become 30 per cent of the population in 12 to 15 years' time, in other words within 12 to 15 years the Muslims will easily become the rulers of this country?

(f) Is it not true that, when destroying the Hindus, they will not stop to think which Hindu belongs to the Lok Dal,

who is a socialist and who a Congressman (or woman)? Who belongs to the forward castes, who to the backward, or who is a Harijan?

(g) Is it not true that, as soon as they gain power they will destroy the Hindus root and branch as they have done in Pakistan?

(h) Is it not true that Hindus (sic) are prohibited from buying land or settling in Kashmir, whereas Kashmiri Muslims are free to buy land wherever they want in the country.

(i) Is it not true the Christians (sic) have their own homeland or country, Muslims also have their own homeland or country, where they feel secure in every way, but Hindus have not been able to retain their country because under the banner of secularism it has been turned into a dharmshala (hospice)?

(j) Is it not true that while Hindus are in power, Muslims can live safely, but as soon as the Muslims come to power, life will become difficult for Hindus—that is, they will be destroyed?

(k) Is it not true that all Muslim legislators (Members of Parliament) irrespective of the party to which they belong, spend night and day working to further the interests of Muslims where there is not a single Hindu legislator in Delhi who seeks self-interest of the Hindus?

(l) Is it not true that Muslim women, who have been divorced by their husbands are supported through the Wakf board, with funds taken from the government treasury? Which means that maintenance and joy (or lust) filled lives of the Muslims, the majority Hindu community has to bear an additional tax burden?

If these things are true, "then Hindu brothers you must immediately awake—awake while there is still time. And vow to sacrifice your wealth, your body, you are all for the protection of the Hindu people and nation and for the declaration of this country as a nation."[57]

What follows from all this is of course a dread of Muslims and the demand to disarm them by disenfranchisement and deculturisation adopt our names 'our' language 'our' dress what follows is the demand that if Muslims wish to stay on in this country they must learn to live like us (who? this is never clear but in the circumstances it does not seem to matter). '*Hindustan main rahna hai to Ram Ram Kahna Hoga*'. A slogan, that appears to have been very popular with the large section of police and local Hindu population in recent Bhagalpur riots was:

"*Babur ki Santano Jao Pakistan ya Kabristan*" (Descendants of Babur! Go to Pakistan or the graveyard).

The obverse of this vilification of the Muslim is the promotion of a rather different image of the 'Hindu' from that which has most commonly been advertised from colonial times till today. The emphasis in this militant Hindu propaganda is not so much on the non-violent, peaceful tolerant character of the Hindus–though astoundingly, even that proposition remains. It is rather more on how "the Hindus" have been tolerant for too long; they are still too timid; the need of the hour is not tolerance but courage—the Hindus must now claim and now finally they have started claiming, what rightfully is theirs.

If Christians have their own nation and Muslims have their own, why should "the Hindus" not have their own nation, their own country, their own state is the only territory they inhabit, where they form an absolute majority and where they have lived for thousands of years? For too long "Hindus" have been asked to make concessions on the grounds of their tolerance and on the plea of 'secularism', they must be bullied no longer, they must make no further concessions. *Garva se kaho hum Hindu hain* (say with pride that you are Hindu) and *Hindu jaaga, desh Jaagega* ("The Hindus awaken, the nation shall awake") as the walls of Delhi and other north Indian cities proclaimed loudly over the last few years.[58]

Sectarian violence in the 1980s appears to have taken on new and increasingly horrifying forms. Recent strife between people belonging to different religious denominations has not been restricted to pitched battles on the streets or cloak and dagger attacks and murders in side lanes, which were the chief markers of earlier riots. The worst instances of recent violence—Bhagalpur in 1989, Meerut in 1987, the anti-Sikh riots in 1984 the anti-Tamil riots in Colombo in 1983, the Hindu-Muslim riots in Moradabad in 1980 and others have amounted to pogroms, massacres in which large crowds of hundreds, thousands and in places, even tens of thousands have attacked the houses and property and lives of small isolated and previously identified members of the other community.[59]

If at first one or two deaths occur in an incident now, as a local leader of the Communist Party of India (Marxist) observed in Bhagalpur, it is not even considered a riot.[60] Attacks on young and old, the blind and the maimed, women, children and infants, the aim of wiping out the enemy and hence physical destruction (of lives, property tools for work and standing crops) are on a massive scale. The unashamed participation of the police, the lynching of people found in trains or buses passing through the affected area, all these have become standard features of today's communal riots.

When the lynching of railway passengers first occurred on a large scale in 1947, it was remarked that as the country had been divided, two new states are coming into being and they needed time to consolidate their positions, the armed forces and police had also been split, confusion, serious crime and violence was almost inevitable. When such actions were repeated in 1984 it was said that a world leader and enormously popular prime minister had been assassinated and when a colossus falls some upheaval, some exceptional reaction is only natural. Now it has become unnecessary to plead exceptional circumstances when people are lynched or burned alive in the course of sectarian strife.

After analysing the events of Delhi riots in 1984 and Bhagalpur riots in 1989, it is proved that violence has become part of the system. Since the 1980s police and media have openly shown their tilt towards a particular community; it is not that before the 1980s the media and police were completely secular but they played a covert role which did not bring them in the limelight and they were considered a part of the solution. But from 1984 and in 1989 it has become part of the problem. It has been established that media and police have shown their affiliation to particular negative tendencies which go against the ethics of their profession.

We have chosen media and police from state agencies to study their role in instigating and flaring communal violence. Why we take these two particular instruments of state is because the media is the means of mass communication, it is the vehicle of change which is entrusted with the very important role of social change. It is the only means through which a popular culture is spread to the far and interior corners of the country. Therefore, the role of the media in communal riots needs special attention to combat communalism.

Ever since the history of communal violence, incidents have been noticed which bear a negative mark on the attitude of police towards minorities. Communalisation of police is a serious point of discussion because during riots police is the first agency which is directly responsible to handle the communal violence. It has a direct bearing on communal incidence.

The state has openly used government organs like Doordarshan and All India Radio to cater to the religious needs of particular religious groups and to spread religiosity, irrationalism and superstitious beliefs.

Communalism has penetrated the very instruments which the state used to contain it. Media has become a tool in the hands of the state, it propagates the policies of the state. Media has played a very partial role, it acts as a custodian of state policies while on the other hand media as a means of communication can be used for building healthy public opinion in favour of secularism and decommunalising the whole edifice. But it needs a political will to eradicate this monster. Media is the medium that shakes up and unsettles the public mind. In India this has been under total government control.[61] In a riot situation and unrest only the government's view or views are telecast, making the coverage one-sided and untrue. The ordinary viewer, however is not immediately able to detect this misinformation.[62]

In actual fact, though there is little evidence that newspapers have occasioned any socially pre-emptive steps over the years, the riot-punctuated areas remain as seismic as ever and the causes are constant as they are frustrating—loud music in front of mosques or temples, provocatively intolerant speeches and carefully engineered rumours. The number of incidents go up year by year and the only antidote that the rulers seem to know is to look upon communal and ethnic riots as a law and order matter and bring the rioters to heel by deploying more and more police, para-military and even military forces. From time to time it is alleged people in the forces themselves are swayed by communal passion and take it out on the people they are supposed to protect. The bigger powers have little or no hand in curbing, checking, diverting or re-educating communal interests.

As in most reporting of conflict, the views of officialdom get much more space. This is not simply because the reporters of national papers stick close to the law and order authorities for their safety or because of their personal views but also because the police, the magistrates and the bureaucratic administration are more accessible. The militants and terrorists are more often underground and have to be reached through subterranean channels. Therefore coverage gives a sharp profile image to the public, the security and para-military forces and to the administration. In Punjab, the Director General of Police's own views are often and fully reported, as are the governor's in Kashmir. At the national level the views of the country's Home Minister and Prime Minister are reported but not the reaction their opinions evoke among the rebels or even among the public.[63]

What we have found with the Indian press is that the act of information is a value-laden process, the emphasis given to specific developments, the tone and content of the coverage of an event by the press reflecting a certain implicit ordering of social priorities. A certain kind of coverage of events may reflect no more than a set of assumptions by media professionals about the range of interests of their leadership.

The print media has shown itself to be insensitive to the loss of human life, except if those involved are upper caste, Hindu urbanities. The Hindu-Muslim animosity is in some senses taken for granted as a substratum of Indian nationalist sentiment, coverage of communal riots tends to be no more than a regurgitation of tired and discredited formulae.[64] For about a century now, Hindu-Muslim animosity has been understood in terms of very superficial determinants—music before mosques, cow slaughter or elopement of a Hindu girl with a Muslim boy or vice versa—in short, the assertion of a religious identity that clashes with the precepts of the other religion. And for a century again, well intentioned but naive commentators have been arguing that both communities should refrain from muting the others' sentiments through too aggressive an assertion of its rituals.

In September 1989, a communal fire was lit in the northern region of the country, which raged on for three months, destroying perhaps 400 lives. There is some uncertainty regarding the exact death toll since the press was rather lax in its accountancy. Kota in Rajasthan and Badaun in Uttar Pradesh exploded in the month of September 1989—these two conflagrations claimed perhaps 50 lives between them. In the first two weeks of October the fire simmered across various small towns in Gujarat, Madhya Pradesh, Rajasthan and even as far afield as Hospet in Karnataka, claiming lives at the rate of one or two every day. It flared up in Indore on October 14, claiming over 40 lives. It then spread slowly across the Hindi heartland, neglected by the state, ignored by the press and fanned by prejudice, until it broke out violently again in Bihar.[66]

Unfortunately both the state and the ruling party were tacitly encouraging the hysteria in the hope of garnering a majoritarian tide of votes in the elections ahead. What was the action of the media? How concerned was the national English language press at these developments.[67]

The results were interesting—between November 1-17, 1989, when the communal riots sparked off by the brick worship rituals claimed over 3000 lives, *The Indian Express* devoted to these killings 610 col-cm of space on its front page and 548 col-cm off the front page. The picture in terms of visual coverage was an abysmal 50 col-cm on the front page and 50 col-cm off the front page. *The Times of India,* despite its tall editorial rhetoric on the scourge of communalism, actually lagged behind, allotting a mere

536 col-cm on the front page and 329 col-cm off the front page to news coverage of the riots. In terms of visual coverage however, it could claim a slight advantage over *The Indian Express*.

Further, with the L.K. Advani motorcade, garishly bedecked in the manner of a Bombay mythological—cutting a swath through Gujarat, Maharashtra and Andhra Pradesh, there was a noticeable increase in the communal temperature in the first week of October 1990. Trivial incidents in Gujarat, Karnataka and Rajasthan exploded into murderous riots, between September 30 to October 4, these riots claimed over 70 lives in places as far afield as Kolar and Channapatna in Karnataka, Baroda in Gujarat, Udaipur in Rajasthan and Gonda in Uttar Pradesh. The figures bear that since these five days of communal riots claimed more than 1000 lives.[68]

What was media's reaction to this instance and how did they cover the incident? *The Indian Express* devoted between October 1 and 5, 153 col-cm of space entirely off the front page to the coverage of these incidents. Visual and editorial coverage was non-existent. *The Times of India* did somewhat worse, its tall editorial rhetoric on religious fanaticism being again unmatched by adequate news coverage of its manifestations. It managed, however to sheathe in a monumentally pompous editorial entitled "Nation in Peril" in which it flaunted its object loyal to the Congress (I) and displayed the opportunistic productivity to blame Prime Minister V.P. Singh for all the ills affecting the nation.

The Press has played a totally irresponsible role in its reporting of communal disturbance, instead of providing insights to the real causes it has provided the public with eyewash reports which is evident from the following incidents.

The Times of India reported the causes of communal disturbance in Palampur, Gujarat in October 1989 that the group clashes and large-scale violence mysteriously started in the afternoon and soon spread to the entire township. The cause of the riots could not be immediately ascertained, but some eye-witnesses attributed it to a quarrel between two rickshaw pullers over Ram Shila (*The Times of India*, October 6, 1989). Or take this story datelined Kota. The violence was triggered when some people stoned the procession being take out by members of another community. And the *Indian Express* reported on November 12, 1989 that the celebrations of Ram Shilanyas in Shimoga irked members of another community who went on a stabbing spree, killing one and injuring seven others.

In its additional comment, *The Indian Express* took an unabashedly majoritation view. Its editor, Arun Shourie did not, however come out with any signed articles expounding his position. He chose instead to hide behind the veil of anonymity, provided by the editorial columns. The contrast could not be sharper, with his performance during the anti-Mandal disturbances, when he came out with at least eight inflammatory articles written in characteristically vain glorious style.[69]

In its anxiety to absolve the Rampujaris of all blame, *The Indian Express* found a convenient scapegoat in the administrations of the district affected between October and November 1989.

Earlier, in an editorial of October 27, *The Indian Express* had called upon the Vishwa Hindu Parishad to postpone its march to Ayodhya, to commence the construction of a temple at the site of the Babri Masjid. But it remained steadfastly unwilling to place on the VHP any part of the blame for the communal disturbances.

After the conclusion of the Shilanyas on November 9, *The Indian Express*'s editorial tone was little short of ghoulish. "The Shilanyas of Ram Mandir in Ayodhya is an important announcement", it crowed, "The Hindus", it chortled "will not put up with reverse discrimination any longer."

The Times of India (TOI) was more subtle and insidious. In its editorial of October 26, it agreed that in every case rioting was a sequel to the Ramshila processions in which participants carried lethal weapons, raised provocative slogans and in short ensured that a clash became inevitable. Unlike *The Indian Express* the *TOI* was not a slave to the majoritatarian illusion. But all the progressive garnishing to its editorial rhetoric proved deceptive, no more than a means of pushing its by now familiar view that the Congress (I) and the Gandhi dynasty are indispensable for the country.

This is the other face of the ideology of indivisible Hindutva with its highly personalised politics centred around a particular dynasty, its denial of the principles of Indian federalism and its rigidly centralised unpopular character.[70] The Congress (I) embodies the monolithic nationalism that is implicit in the idea of the Hindu Rashtra. Over the ten years of the Indira-Rajiv Raj, the Congress (I) patented and propagated a notion of national unity, that is in conflict with the liberty and well-being of the nation's citizens and the autonomy and integrity of its political institutions. Because of its strongly entrenched character of a personality cult, the Congress (I) is by nature averse to all forms of political mobilisation except those with a majoritarian orientation.

Thus, while Prime Minister Rajiv Gandhi and the discredited bunch of time servers who surround him, maintained a cynical silence on the communal killings, the *TOI* chose to direct its editorial ire against the opposition parties. On October 14, it proclaimed that the time has finally come for all political parties to stand up and counter forces of Hindutva. On October 17, its tone was that of abject devotion towards a political master. It is surely for the Prime Minister to take a lead role in dealing with the matter. He cannot allow electoral calculations to distract him from the vital mission of ensuring communal peace in the country.

Later, as it became apparent that the then Prime Minister Mr. Rajiv Gandhi, was indeed pandering to religious fanaticism to foster his vote bank, the *TOI* became in turn plaintive and accusing—plaintive towards Rajiv Gandhi, accusing towards the opposition parties. In its editorial of October 21, 1989, it argued that the Congress promotion of Hindu revivalism was regrettable, but the electoral understanding being worked out by the Janta Dal and the CPI (M) were respectively pathetic and tragic.

In a gesture of surpassing cynicism, Rajiv Gandhi inaugurated his election campaign at Ayodhya on November 3, 1989, with the promise to usher in a Ram Rajya if re-elected. By then it was clear that the secular force was on the other foot. It was V.P. Singh who was making the more definitive statements on Ayodhya. It was V.P. Singh who was offering to go to the disputed site on November 9, to try and stop the threatened demolition of a place of worship. But the *TOI* was firm in its editorial policy of unrequited love towards Rajiv Gandhi as the following excerpt from its editorial of November 7 shows. "It is still not too late for Mr. Rajiv Gandhi to call the VHP's bluff. Even today it is possible for Mr. Rajiv Gandhi to set aside momentarily his electoral preoccupation and go along with his political adversaries in order to defuse the tensions building up at Ayodhya."[71]

After the completion of Ram Shilanyas at Ayodhya on November 9, the *TOI*'s editorial sigh of relief could be heard for miles around. It was now possible to be a lap dog of Congress (I) while still maintaining a pretence of secularism. In an astonishing display of political amnesia, the *TOI* proclaimed editorially that the foundation stone-laying ceremony would not have passed off as peacefully as it did had the Chief Minister of Uttar Pradesh, Mr. N.D. Tiwari fully backed by the Union Home Minister, Mr. Buta Singh not worked assiduously behind the scenes (November 10, 1989). Curiously, Rajiv Gandhi was around the same time making the breathtakingly mendacious assertion that the 'credit' for the peaceful passage of the foundation stone-laying cermony at Ayodhya should go to his party and its government. The question here arises why was not his party so keen on owning up responsibility for the 400 lives that had been lost in the run-up to the Shilanyas?

The Congress (I) stands condemned for its role in fermenting the Babri Masjid-Ramjanambhoomi controversy for narrow electoral gains. Astoundingly, of all the parties that today dot the Indian political firmament the Congress (I) is the only one without a position on the Ayodhya issue.[72]

In following and reporting contemporary events like Punjab, Kashmir, Mandal, Ramjanambhoomi-Babri Masjid, the news weeklies like *Economic and Political Weekly, Social Scientist, Mainstream, Muslim India* and *Seminar* did a better and more intelligent job. They are fighting an ideological battle against state and communalism by analysing and generating public opinion. They also seem to be relatively free of official influence. Their interviews are pointed and they make an effort to reach and report rebel views which the public needs to know in order to arrive at a judgement.[73]

Communalisation of Police

In situations of communal tension or conflict, the police is expected to be part of the solution. Tragically, during the 1980s, it seems it has become a part of the problem in many areas. How can communalism be kept in check if the police itself turns communal?[74]

According to the National Police Commission report in March 1981 which wrote about communalisation of police in two paragraphs, the first para stated, "we also heard of stringent criticism from many responsible quarters that the police do not often act with impartiality and objectivity. Several instances have been cited where police officers and men appear to have shown unmistakable bias against a particular community while dealing with communal situations. Serious allegations of high handedness and other atrocities, including such criminal activities as arson and looting, molestation of women, etc. have been levelled against the police deployed to protect the citizens."[75]

The other para stated, "the Madon commission which inquired into the communal riots in Bhiwandi, Jalgaon and Mahad in the state of Maharashtra in 1969 passed severe structures against the special investigation squads set up to investigate crimes committed in the course of these riots. The commission observed that these squads had acted in the partial and biased manner against one community."[76]

November 1984 has changed the picture. Following Indira Gandhi's assassination, rampaging mobs fell upon the Sikhs in Delhi and some other places. Thousands of innocent Sikhs were killed. Property worth crores was looted or burnt, dozens of gurudwaras glutted and unspeakable brutalities committed such as the burning of young boys. The policemen either looked the other way or worse incited the mobs to even more violence. During the three days of that horror, the police was certainly not on the side of the angels.[77]

Then came the ghastly happenings of May 1987 in and around Meerut where UP's Provincial Armed Constabulary (PAC) killed scores of innocent Muslims of Hashimpura and Malliana. Nikhil Chakravarty wrote in *Mainstream*, "something has happened in Meerut which has never happened in this country. It has now come to be known that at a certain place the PAC gangs suddenly descended, knocked and burst into the hutments of poor Muslims picked up whoever they could grab (mainly the young) packed them off into PAC trucks and lined them up. They then shot them down and threw the dead bodies into the river."

The points to note are that first, those picked up and packed off were not culprits involved in rioting and killing but were victims of an indiscriminate round-up of all and sundry. Second, there was absolutely no pretence of bringing them to justice or detaining them but to kill them in cold blood and dispose of their corpses.[78]

Policemen in Meerut actively planned and carried out a cold-blooded massacre of blameless Muslims. In a classic understatement the Gian Prakash committee pointed out that this had shaken the confidence of the minority community in the administrative machinery. The truth is that Hashimpura and Malliana affected the Muslim psyche as nothing else had since Independence, for the community began to see itself under attack by the state itself.

Since the 1987 Meerut riots, Muslims all over India have lost faith in the police, when communalisation of police came into light in 1987. So, Muslims now do not consider PAC as their protector. The least that should have been done was to have promptly disbanded this particular unit of the PAC and to have cashiered its officers. But no action was taken. The outcome was that far from being on the side of the angels the UP police emerged as the devil itself.[79]

Reports from Bhagalpur (October 1989) indicate that the Bihar police has out-devilled the PAC of UP. The Bihar Military Police (BMP), the general police and the Income Guards were reported to have joined the marauders. Instead of providing protection to the panic-stricken families and moving them to safe localities, the police beat them up indiscriminately.[80] A group of Muslims, rescued by the Army and left under police protection overnight, were allowed to be butchered through deliberate action. Criminals from the Diara belt were able to join forces with local hoodlums to perpetrate massacre after massacre. Even families of Muslim policemen under police protection were allowed to be killed. As a result a new phenomenon emerged : policemen could no longer trust each other. A BSF officer told *Frontline,* "I have been posted all over India and I have never seen such a corrupt sadistic and inefficient police force as Bihar."[81]

The National Police Commission reports (1981), Delhi (1984), Meerut (1987) and Bhagalpur (1989) illustrate the descent of the police from the protective instrument it was meant to be to the dangerous communal beast it has tended to become in times of crisis. Obviously the state cannot remain secular if its law and order machinery becomes communal. Equally, it cannot remain democratic if it ceases to be secular.[82]

The 1980s have been marked by an upsurge of communal feelings. Inevitably this has found reflection in the police. Communalisation of police and that too of Hindu variety needs an explanation, which also means that there is a shift in the attitude of society where the Hindu military is getting nurtured.

According to L.K. Advani, Hindu chauvinism in recent years has been in response to Muslim fundamentalism, to Sikh seclusion, to the Meenakshipuram conversions and to the passage of the Muslim Women (protection of Rights of Divorce) Act 1986. All the above factors and organised propagation of VHP in 1980 led to the revivalism of Hindutva.

The machinery of the state for maintaining internal security, is composed of the normal police, the armed police of the state, such as UP's PAC and Bihar's BMP paramilitary forces of the union, mainly the Central Reserve Police Force (CRPF) and the Border Security Force (BSF) and ultimately the Armed Forces, nearly always the army.

The army has an enviable record of dealing with civil disorder including communal unrest, in an impartial, effective and humane manner. Punjab and the North-East are special cases which stand out as warnings of what overuse can do to even the army in terms of lowering its sensitivity to the employment of inhuman methods and allowing communal attitudes to creep in. A time was when district officers felt that asking for Army help was tantamount to an admission of failure. But 'aid to civil power' has now become so routine as to sound alarm bells. Frequent resort to the military not only reflects poorly on the normal law and order machinery but is also not so good for the army. Nevertheless, Imam Bhukari's tribute to the army in the Bhagalpur riots is worth quoting, *"Military muhafiz bani, police qatil bani"* (military was the protector while the police turned killer).[84]

The record of the Union's paramilitary forces is mixed. In a study of the 1969 communal riots in Ahmedabad, Ghanshyam Shah concluded that the police had utterly failed in its duty of maintaining law and order impartially. At several places, killing and looting took place in the presence of policemen. Often SRP and CRP cadets were told that Muslims needed such treatment.[85] The SRP (State Reserve Police), observed Asghar Ali Engineer about the 1981 Vadodara riot, played the same role as the PAC played in Moradabad and Meerut. Read together, these remarks would suggest that the CRPF is no better than Gujarat's SRP or UP's PAC.[86] But while going into the 1981 Bihar Sharif communal killings, Asghar Ali Engineer[87] also said, it was a common complaint that the Bihar Military police abetted the goondas in looting and burning properties and killing people. The victims testified before that but for the arrival of the BSF and the CRP, the toll of life and property in Bihar Sharif would have been much higher. The BSF and CRP deployed maintained remarkable impartiality in handling the situation and saved many lives and properties.

A panel discussion organised by the National Police Academy at Hyderabad on communal violence confirmed a fact based on the statement made by a senior police officer from a northern state that a political interference rendered the handling of communal unrest difficult. Against this, an inspector general from Karnataka stated that in his experience "nobody had stopped a police officer faced with a communal situation, from doing what he thought was right and proper". Much the same was said by a senior policeman from West Bengal. The discussion confirmed what is well known otherwise, that the communalisation of the police is certainly not an India-wide phenomenon. The seriously affected states, not counting Punjab are five: UP, Bihar, Madhya Pradesh, Gujarat and Maharashtra.[88]

The fact is that the communal virus has made dangerous inroads into police impartiality in these states. What is worse, the communal attitudes of Hindu policemen seem to have sanction, vocal or silent, of important sections of Hindu society. The combination of communalised police and societal sanction could prove deadly, literally so for Muslims and metaphorically for the values proclaimed in the Constitution.

Half the Muslims in India live in just three states—UP, Bihar and West Bengal. Against the national ratio of 11.4 per cent Muslims are almost 16 per cent in UP, 14 per cent in Bihar and as many as 21.5 per cent in West Bengal. While the communal situation in UP and Bihar is near boiling point with a communalised police pitching in with its own contribution, West Bengal enjoys communal harmony barring small incidents here and there. So much so that Muslims fleeing from Bhagalpur have sort refuge in West Bengal. Many West Bengal policemen hail from UP and Bihar, yet the police in that state has a reputation for impartiality and effectiveness in handling communal situations.[89]

The question of making the police more effective in dealing with communal and caste riots had been examined by the National Police Commission and it has suggested several measures. Ironically politicians in power, in their own interest do not want the implementation of the recommendations of the commission. Sincere efforts and encouragement of political leaders who are truly above communal taint can and will reform police.

The communalisation of body polity had been increasing during the years but in the 1980s there was an unprecedented rise of communal violence. The study of the communal riots reveals certain salient features including sudden, spontaneous and abrupt outbursts due to penetration of communal ideology followed by a systematic planning, emergence and rise of lumpen elements in politics as well as communal riots, protection given by the police and politicians, active role by the communal organisations and communal elements amongst the secular parties, communal outlook of the administrative set-up and the policy of hide and seek. The emergence of the most powerful and dangerous police-politicians-bureaucracy and underworld nexus also perpetrate communal riots.

The study of communal riots in post-Independence India indicates that communalisation is an ever increasing phenomenon and a condition or 'psyche' which is the result of a number of factor including increasing religiosity, the use of communal symbols, religious processions and congregations, economic rivalries and competition for jobs, urbanisation and lack of accommodation, poverty, hunger and employment, jealousy for employment and promotion. But what has been a marked trend during 1980 is the organised violence encouraged by government to divert the attention of the people from economic issues, communalised politics, non-functioning of our political institutions frequent use of military and other paramilitary organisations like PAC, BSF, CRPF, etc. to curb political agitations and agitations from economic issues, politicians bureaucracy, police and underworld nexus, misuse of religious places for communal propaganda as well as anti-social, anti-national and immoral and irreligious activities, non-resolving of sensitive issues like Ram Janambhoomi, Babri Masjid, clustering of religious and caste groups non-absorption of workers, etc. As a result, the entire body polity has been highly charged with communal powder keg and a small incident like hot argument among the members of different communities can create serious trouble.

REFERENCES

1. Wayne A. Wilcox, *Political Modernisation in South Asia,* California: Rand Corporation, 1968, p. 12.
2. Bipan Chandra, "Communalism: The Way Out-1", *The Hindustan Times*, June 1, 1987, p. 9.
3. A.R. Saiyed, "Changing Urban Ethos: Some Reflections on Hindu-Muslim Riots", in K.S. Shukla (ed.), *Collective Violence: Genesis*

and Responses, New Delhi: Indian Institute of Public Administration, 1988, p. 98.

4. Ibid., p. 99.
5. P.R. Rajagopal, *Communal Violence in India*, New Delhi: Uppal Publishing House, 1987, pp. 16-17.
6. Studies conducted by Institute of Islamic Studies, Bombay; Centre for Research in Rural and Industrial Development, Chandigarh, 1959, pp. 79-80.
7. Raghubir Dayal Report of the Commission of Inquiry into the Communal Disturbances, Ranchi-Hatia, August 22-29, 1967, Delhi: Central Government Press, 1968.
8. A.A. Engineer, *Communalism and Communal Violence: An Analytical Approach to Hindu-Muslim Conflict,* Delhi: Ajanta Publications, 1989.
9. Ibid., p. 109.
10. Raghubir Dayal Commission of Inquiry Report on Ranchi Riots, August 1968.
11. A.A. Engineer, "On the Theory of Communal Riots", in A.A. Engineer and Moin Shakir (eds.), *Communalism in India*, Delhi: Ajanta Publications, 1985.
12. A.A. Engineer on the Ahmedabad Riots.
13. Moin Shakir, *State and Politics in Contemporary India*, Delhi: South Asia Books, 1986, p. 184.
14. Ibid., p. 186.
15. Ibid., p. 187.
16. Op. cit., Raghubir Dayal Report.
17. A.R. Saiyed, op. cit., p. 99.
18. Ibid., p. 102.
19. Ratna Naidu, *Communal Edge to Plural Society*, New Delhi: Vikas Publishing House, 1980, p. 146.
20. Quoted in Hussain Shaheen, "Communal Riots in the Post-Partition Period in India: A Study of Some Causes and Remedial Measures", in A.A. Engineer (ed.), *Communal Riots in Post Independence India*, Hyderabad: Sangam Books, 1984, p. 171.
21. Ibid., p. 174.
22. Moin Shakir, *State and Politics in Contemporary India*, Delhi: Ajanta Publications, 1986, p. 172.
23. A.A. Engineer, "Politician and Communal Violence", *The Hindustan Times*, November 6, 1989.
24. Ashwani Ray, "Communal Politics and Communal Violence",

Mainstream, September 1981, p. 53.

25. Imtiaz Ahmad, "Communal Riots in India", *The Times of India*, December 1, 1987.
26. Ibid.
27. Rajni Kothari, "Communalism in India: The New Face of Democracy", *Lokayan Bulletin*, New Delhi, June 3, 1985, p. 56.
28. Ibid., p. 59.
29. Rajni Kothari, *State Against Democracy*, Delhi: Ajanta Publications, 1987, p. 253.
30. Rajni Kothari, *Police and the People*, Delhi: Ajanta Publications, 1989, p. 439.
31. Rajni Kothari, op. cit., 1987, p. 263.
32. PUCL Report on Delhi Riots, "Who are the guilty?", New Delhi, 1984, p. 4.
33. Ibid., p. 5.
34. Nikhil Chakravarty, "Congress (I) and Communalism", *Deccan Herald*, November 14, 1989.
35. Op. cit., PUCL Report, New Delhi, p. 17.
36. PUCL Report, Delhi Riots, p. 20.
37. Rajni Kothari, op. cit., 1987, p. 258
38. Ibid., p. 279
39. Rajni Kothari, "Cultural Context of Communalism", *Radical Humanist*, Vol. 54, No. 1, April 1990, p. 42.
40. Ibid., p. 186.
41. PUDR Report, Bhagalpur Riots, Delhi, April 1990, p. 70.
42. Gyanendra Pandey, *The Construction of Communalism in Colonial North India*, New Delhi: Oxford University Press, 1990, p. 5.
43. PUDR Report, op. cit., 1990, p. 17.
44. This whole passage is based on the reports of PUDR, p. 45, and newspapers during that period.
45. Ibid., p. 47.
46. Ibid., p. 24.
47. Ibid.
48. Gyanendra Pandey, "In Defence of the Fragment: Writing About Hindu-Muslim Riots in India Today", *Economic and Political Weekly*, Vol. 26, No. 11/12, Annual Number, March 1991, pp. 559-572.
49. Partik Kanjilal, "Bhagalpur: The Scars That Remain", *Statesman*, October 27, 1990.
50. Shantimay Roy, "Bhagalpur Carnage in Perspective", *Mainstream*, Vol. 28 (20), March 10, 1990, pp. 15, 17, 28.

51. PUDR Report on Bhagalpur Riots, p. 1.
52. This was the rumour which sparked off the riots in Bhagalpur, but no investigation was conducted by the State Government but still this news was aired by the Radio and was covered by all the newspapers.
53. Op. cit., A.A. Engineer, 1985.
54. PUDR Report on Bhagalpur Riots, p. 65.
55. Ibid., p. 43.
56. Hindu Bandhuon, Socho aur Sambhlo, (by Rajeshwar, Akhil Bharat Hindu Mahasabha), Translated by Gyanendra Pandey is the reproduction of the content of pamphlet no. 54.
57. Pamphlet by Vishwa Hindu Parishad entitled "Chetanvani Desh Ko Khatra", New Delhi.
58. *The Times of India* (Lucknow edition), August 13, 1990.
59. Gyanendra Pandey, op. cit., 1991, p. 570.
60. Ibid., p. 572.
61. K.N. Panikkar (ed.), *Communalism in India*, New Delhi: Manohar Publications, 1990, p. 15.
62. Chanchal Sarkar, "Communal Divide", *Seminar*, October 90, Issue No. 374. p. 25.
63. Ibid., p. 26.
64. Charu and Mukul, "Hindi Language Press and Bhagalpur Riots", *Mainstream*, Vol. 28, No. 20, March 10, 1990, pp. 18-20.
65. Ibid., p. 10.
66. P. Sainath, "Press and Communalism", *Social Scientist*, Vol. 18, March, 1990, pp. 158-60.
67. Charu and Mukul, op. cit., 1990, p. 19.
68. For this analysis, number of editorials and articles have been chronologically studied by P. Sainath in "Press and Communalism", *Social Scientist*, March 1990, pp. 158-172.
69. Ibid., p. 17.
70. Arun Shourie, *Indian Express*, November 12, 1989.
71. K.N. Panikkar, op. cit., p. 29.
72. Editorial, *The Times of India*, November 7, 1989.
73. Syed Shahabuddin, "Rajiv and Ram Rajya", *Muslim India*, Vol. 105, Delhi, September 1991, p. 29.
74. Chanchal Sarkar, op. cit., p. 29.
75. Nirmal Mukherjee, "Communal Divide"; Who Will Guard the Guards?" *Seminar* (374), October 1990, pp. 14-17.
76. S.K. Ghosh, op. cit., p. 143.

77. Ibid., pp. 162-63.
78. B.K. Sharma, "Communalisation of the Indian Police: Causes, Consequences and Remedies", *Political Science Review*, 27 (1-4); 1988, p. 155.
79. Ibid., p. 125.
80. A.A. Engineer (ed.), *Secularism and the Emerging Challenge of Communalism: Practical Aspects in Delhi-Meerut Riots*, Delhi: Ajanta Publications, 1988, p. 172.
81. A.A. Engineer, "Grim Tragedy of Bhagalpur Riots: Role of Police-Criminal Nexus", *Economic and Political Weekly*, Vol. 25, No. 6, February 10, 1990, pp. 305-307.
82. Ibid., p. 306.
83. PUDR Report, Role of Police: Bhagalpur Riots, New Delhi, 1990, p. 17.
84. See the Section in this chapter on Bhagalpur Riots, where organised propaganda by VHP, RSS has been discussed.
85. Nirmal Mukherjee, op. cit., p. 18.
86. A.A. Engineer, op. cit., p. 281.
87. Ibid., p. 286.
88. Ibid., p. 238.
89. S.K. Ghosh, op. cit., pp. 91-92.
90. Nirmal Mukherjee, op. cit., p. 15.
91. J.R. Siwach, *Dynamics of Indian Government and Politics*, New Delhi: Sterling Publishers, 1985, pp. 488-89.
92. P.R. Rajagopal, "How Violence Has Grown", *The Hindustan Times*, August 21, 1987, p. 9.

5

COMMUNALISM TO FASCISM

The communal carnage carried out in Gujarat after February 27, 2002 was an expression of majoritarian communalism nurtured, developed and consolidated by the Hindutva forces in civil society, winning substantial support or response among Hindus, and having the open support, assistance and participation by the BJP government, administration and police. During the emergency, a vibrant civil society resisted state power, but in Gujarat, the communalised state acted in close collaboration with the supporting or sympathetic Hindus in large numbers, remaining silent or passive Hindu society, and Muslims were the targets. Once the polity is controlled by the Sangh Parivar and the civil society is substantially communalised in terms of 'We' and 'They' and 'they' are identified with international Islam, Pakistan and terrorism branded as anti-national, the threat is more open, direct, serious and dangerous for the forces of democracy, rule of law, secularism, social justice and pluralism.[1]

The Hindutva ideology of the RSS Parivar, namely, India is Hindu and Hinduism is nationalism, subscribing to the Hindu state, which is described as national mainstream or cultural nationalism, in which Muslims and Christians are minorities and second class citizens and can live only if they win the goodwill of the majority, cannot be implemented in India through the constitutional system. Both cannot co-exist. And therefore the Gujarat situation is a direct subversion of the constitution and presents a permanent threat, which if not defeated, will destroy the constitution itself.[2]

The riots in Gujarat in which so many lives have been lost, are perhaps, independent India's worst riots, both in terms of numbers and brutality of killing. More than two and a half months of continuing violence have sent shock waves across the globe. What is not disputed is the fact that two coaches of the Sabarmati Express were attacked and set afire by a mob at Godhra and that the violence ultimately led to the burning alive of 58 Hindu Karsevaks, who were returning from Ayodhya. Most of the dead were women and children. Even as the Godhra tragedy was roundly condemned, the anticipated backlash took the dimensions of a holocaust primarily aimed at the Muslim community. It is also not disputed that in the following weeks Ahmedabad and Bawda, and many villages and towns of Vadodara Panchmahal, Mahasana and Sabarkantha witnessed unusual mob frenzy. According to official accounts the death toll crossed 900, whereas according to unofficial assessment it ranges from 2000 to 5000. Men, women and children killed mercilessly, many even burnt alive.[3]

Property worth hundreds of crores was destroyed, Darghas and mosques have been destroyed. Some of them have been converted to temples, attacks were organised by the VHP and the Bajrang Dal who had earlier gathered information on minority houses, shops, etc. The attacks were planned accordingly, with first looting, and then burning of shops and establishments along with brutal violence stabbing and battering and even burning people alive with kerosene, petrol and diesel.

It was also alleged that there were sexual assaults on women and gangrape in the presence of their relatives. The brutalities were unprecedented especially against women.The targeting of Muslim homes, establishments and sources of livelihood was precise and bears evidence of premeditation. The term "ethnic cleansing" and genocide have been used to describe the horror. There is no disagreement that loss of every kind has mainly been suffered by Muslims.

This communal project also becomes clear from the fact that Muslims from all the sections of the population, from slum dwellers to businessmen and white-collar professionals to senior government bureaucrats were targeted during the attacks, even the upper middle class sections of the Muslim community were targeted. The Delite and Tarana Apartments of the Muslim flat owners were completely gutted and the belongings of these multistoreyed apartments looted. The residents included the Director of Industries, Gujarat government and a senior employee of the Gujarat University.[4]

Frantic phone calls to ministers, ruling party politicians and even to politicians in Delhi could not prevent the total destruction of the apartments by a 5,000 strong mob which broke open into the flats and ransacked them. The residents were able to avoid the fate of Eashan Jaffery (former Congress MP) who was burnt alive in Gulmarg Society by hiding in the terrace of the building and not raising their voice even when the mobs went on a rampage inside their homes. They could not conceal their deep hurt while recollecting that many people from their neighbouring apartments whom they had known and lived together with for several years, not only cheered the rioters during the operation but some actually participated in it.[5]

Gujarat experienced a new and novel form of violence. Burning of people alive in a systematic and gruesome manner is new. As many as two people out of nearly a thousand seem to have been killed in this way. The mode of violence derives its logic and legitimacy from the overall framework within which violence is conceived and justified when violence is not interpersonal but intercommunal and part of one community's collective hostility against another, as was the case in Gujarat. Burning people alive has sinister advantages and a macabre logic not available to the usual forms of killing. It can be easily executed by organised groups with tacit support or acquiescence of their community, used to wipe out large numbers indiscriminately, poses no danger to the perpetrators and helps to create an internal climate of terror.

All these eerie experiences point towards a tremendous communalisation of society that has taken place in Ahmedabad and other places of Gujarat. Hatred towards the Muslim minority has been systematically inculcated in such a manner that violence of barbaric proportions against them is not only widely condoned but also even enjoyed by certain sections of the Hindu communities. The press statement issued by noted historian Prof. K.N. Panikkar on 9th March after his visit to Ahmedabad, is thus significant.

> "What happened in Ahmedabad and other towns and villages in Gujarat is not a spontaneous action. The methods used for destruction of life and property presupposes a fairly well organised plan. In a way it indicates a long-term process of communalisation and brutalisation of society. A major issue which society has to face is the influence of brutality, which appears to have conquered the minds of men. This is the result of the systematic and long-term atrocities of communal organisations heightened by the irrational and emotional coercion of the people by both the VHP and the RSS."[5]

The Gujarat carnage is an attack on Indian democracy, its diversity and pluralism. India has been plural, not only since it adopted democracy and became a republic in 1950. India has been plural for ages and it always has been proud of its rich pluralist legacy. Indian pluralism is the anchor of our secularism. We cannot think of our secular democracy without pluralism. It is the Bajrang Dal and RSS people who are never tired of accusing Muslims that they refuse to be a part of the 'Indian mainstream'. This is not true but even if it were, who is responsible for their being out of stream? If they are expelled from government and private schools will they not be taken lightly by those who care about the secular character of Indian democracy, if it happens, even if partially, it will be the beginning of the end of our pluralism and our secular democracy.

What happened in Gujarat is a concerted assault on this pluralism. Muslims are sought to be completely isolated in ghettos and looked down upon as if they were non-Indians. The Vishwa Hindu Parishad and its cohorts distributed pamphlets on a large scale with the blessings of the BJP Government for economic boycott of Muslims—not to sell to them and not to buy from them. The VHP enthusiasts were going round various schools and threatening its headmasters and principals to remove Muslim students from their rolls. It sends a chilling sensation down one's spine to thinking of what would happen if Muslim students are really removed from schools under threat from the VHP and Bajrang Dal. The ghettoisation will be complete.[6]

The other factor, which also should be seriously reflected upon is participation of Dalits and backwards in this genocide on a big scale. Many have emphasised that Dalit Muslims unite to fight communal fascism. But the Hindutvawadis have instilled a sense of Hinduness among Dalits for their misdeeds against Muslims.[7]

The huge crowds of ten to fifteen thousand, which collected and surrounded Muslims, from all sides mostly, consisted of Dalits and the backward. Of course in Gujarat there is no Dalit leadership worth the name. Some who had taken the lead for Dalits during the 1981 anti-Dalit riots have become totally ineffective and Dalits who had shown anger against upper caste Hindus and vowed to fight them have united with them again. They were undoubtedly given liquor and money plus the incentive of loot. But this does not explain the fury with which they attacked.[8]

The constant propaganda against Muslims that they are enemies and anti-nationals and must be taught a lesson also had its effect. The VHP, in order to fight Muslims with the help of Dalits expresses 'solidarity' with them as Hindus and instils in them a strong dose of Hinduness de-emphasising their Dalitness in such a situation. In the political strategy of Hindutva, Dalits support is important not only for Muslims carnage but also to win during elections with their support assigning them a subordinate position.[9]

Gujarat is not prone to communal violence in the sense that it does not tend to occur with distressing regularity, as is evident in the fact that in the past fifty years, Gujarat has enjoyed over thirty years of communal peace. Moreover, when violence does occur, as it did in 1969 and 1992-93, it tends to be extensive and to last longer, giving Gujarat the dubious and double distinction of having the highest per capita deaths in such violence in the country and causing the highest of casualities in a single cluster of riots.[10]

During the recent riots, communalism ran extremely deep and pervaded almost all areas of life. The Gujarati media were grossly biased and even provocative. The government gave up all pretence of neutrality and openly encouraged Hindu violence. It even offered differential compensation to Hindus and Muslims, and wants to try them under different laws, Muslims under POTA and Hindus under IPC. Communalism seems to have spread even to some hospitals in Ahmedabad. And the advocates of intercommunal harmony have not only been thrown on the defensive but positively terrorised into silence.[11]

Violence in Gujarat did not remain confined to the usual cities of *Ahmedabad Baroda* (the 'sanskarnagari' as its citizens have been taught to call it without any sense of embarrassment and irony), but extended to 37 cities and towns and even to some villages that had no previous record of such violence. Even Gandhi Nagar became a victim, where fire was set to the offices of the government Wakf Board and the Minority Development Board.[12]

Violence in Gujarat involved groups that had hitherto kept out of it. These included the adivasis, subjected in recent years to the systematic process of Hinduisation and "protected in their own interest" against Christian and more recently Islamic missionaries, as a VHP leader put it. It was targeted not only against those responsible for the event of 27th February, but against all Muslims. The latter were linked with Pakistan and presented as an internal enemy. The violence against them was driven not so much by communal hatred as in the past but by a dangerous mixture of self-righteous rage and despair, rage that Muslims had engaged in a 'terrorist' act, and despair, that they would never be ours, as a newspaper commentator put it.[13]

Hindus worked themselves into a state of frenzy and resorted to violence, not just in a legitimate self-defence but as an act of patriotism and well deserved chastisement of Muslims for their alleged ingratitude and betrayal. Their violence often lacked instrumental rationality and was devoid of any sense of guilt and remorse. It was not the usual form of communal violence but a veritable war on Muslims, and terrorist in its nature and intention.

Gujarat, which had once given India its doctrine of non-violence, was now the home of a most perverse form of intercommunal violence.

Gujarat was a victory for those who seek to divide the communities into exclusionary ghettos across the country. The Indian state cannot and must not negotitate a 'solution' with the most loutish, intolerant and criminalised elements of a community, and in the shadow of brutal massacres, any such negotiations would strengthen the very forces which engineered the barbarism. The real issue is that of hatred and exclusion and the violent strategies and tactics it adopts for its realisation.[14]

This ideology irrespective of its claimed religious affliation is indistinguishable from the ideologies that led to Indian partition, and that, even today, inspires 'jihad factories'' and its armies of terrorists beyond our border. There is, indeed, no difference between the political groupings that exploit primordial and irrational sentiments constructed around the 'Hindu' identity, and those who have been mobilised by Pakistan's ruling elite to serve the Islamist jihad. The herd that has been formed through the ideology of Hindutva is politically, socially and psychologically indistinguishable from the herd that has been credited through the ideology of extremist Islam.[15] Nor, in fact, despite differences in outward symbols and practices linked to their 'religious identity, are there any real differences in their belief systems.

Communalisaiton of the Police

The role played by the state in general and the civil and police administration is highly provocative. The majority of the Gujarat police was also influenced by the forces of Hindutva and there are evidences which showed that it carried on an agenda of ethnic elimination of Muslims in the state. It has emerged as the *agent provocateur* and active participant in the arson loot, murder and mayhem.[16]

The Police Commissioner of Ahmedabad P.C. Pandey had stated in a TV interview that the police force is part of society and it should not be surprising if it supports the majority community. The Chief Minister of Gujarat Narendra Modi had also said, "Police are human beings as well and not inured to the sentiments of society. The police are equally influenced by the overall general sentiment. "Here we have a top police official being indulgent towards his policemen who somehow get carried away by "general sentiments", when the least that could be expected of him would be a categorical assertion that those in the force who had failed to enforce the rule of law were a disgrace to the uniform they donned and would themselves be punished in accordance with the law.[17]

The partisan role of the police becomes all the more glaring as the Gujarat Police itself admitted that it killed more Muslims than Hindus in its ostensible attempts to stop what was clearly targeted Hindu violence against Muslims. Of the 184 people who died in police firing since the violence began, 104 are Muslims, says a report drafted by the Gujarat police force itself. The statistics substantiate the allegations of riot victims from virtually every part of the state that not only did the local police not do anything to stop the Hindu mobs; they actually turned their guns on the helpless Muslim victims.[18]

The police in Gujarat aided and abetted the rioters. This time the role of IAS officers also came under severe criticism. Harsh Mandar, an IAS officer of the MP cadre working in Gujarat with Actionaid India at that time was so enraged by the role of IAS officers of Gujarat and their total surrender to the political authorities that he did not think it fit to continue in such a service and resigned in sheer disgust. Harsh Mandar wrote in his article, "Numbed with disgust and horror, I return from Gujarat ten days after the terror and massacre that convulsed the state. My heart is sickened, my soul wearied, my shoulders aching with the burden of shame and guilt."[19] He further writes, "The unconscionable failures and active connivance of the state police and administrative machinery is now widely acknowledged. The police have known to have misguided people straight into the hands of rioting mobs. They provided protective shields to crowds bent upon pillage, arson, rape and murder and were deaf to the pleas of these disparate Muslim victims, many of them women and children. There have been many reports of police firing directly mostly at the minority community, which was targeted of most of the mob violence."[20]

The police did not even conduct the mandatory police drill. They did not even follow the basic procedure stipulated for such circumstances. They did not contact religious and community leaders to make appeals for peace, nor take steps to arrest the culprits and give support to the victims. On February the 28th, as carefully planned mass killings were engineered in 30 different locations all over the state, two senior cabinet ministers sat in the police control room in Ahmedabad and the state police control room in Gandhinagar and directly influenced police action, or inaction. The actions and non-actions of the Gujarat police on that day and thereafter, are, barring a few sterling exceptions, proof of the partisan, political control over the police.[21]

The police chiefs of Ahmedabad, Vadodara, Rajkot, Mehsana, Panchmahal, Dahod and Sabakantha stand individually indicted for their failure to control unprecedented violence in their respective jurisdictions. The SPs of several of Gujarat's 24 districts are also directly culpable. The general message sent out to the police was: minimum response to panic calls and minimal action thereafter; indulgence towards armed mobs as they went about their business of killing, rape, loot and arson; either non-registration or tailoring of complaints from victims. It is unpardonable that the police obeyed such unwritten directions from Modi and other political bosses.[22]

As if this were not bad enough, the police itself committed atrocities against Muslims, especially in Vadodara (Bahar Colony, Noor Park and other areas) and Ahmedabad (Gomtipur and elsewhere). In Bapunagar area it is alleged that police killed about 40 young boys at point blank range. As post mortem reports show, the bullets had hit them, on their heads and chests. Many lives were saved just because the military arrived. Otherwise the death toll would have been much higher. And in case of Akbarnagar in Ahmedabad a whole colony was destroyed just behind the office of assistant commissioner of police. Even women were beaten and thrashed, often on their breasts and vaginas. In fact, such widespread sexual misbehaviour of the police with Muslim women marks a new low in police misconduct against the minorities.

Police conduct after the Gujarat carnage, with regard to the registration of crimes, conducting of investigations, etc., has been marked by a desire to please political bosses and an utter disregard for the law of the land. This is nothing but calculated miscarriage of justice. The police are required to file separate FIRs for each incident. Instead, separate incidents of crime committed by different aggressors at different places at different times have been clubbed together in single omnibus FIRs.[24] Panchnamas have either been made 3-4 weeks after the incidents or not at all. Also, if the charge-sheets filed in the Gulberg (Chamapua), Naroda Gaon and Patiya massacres are anything to go by, the names of the main accused have been conveniently dropped. Worse still, in places like Pandharwada, Anjanwa, Mora (Panchmahal district) as well as in villages in Bharuch, Sabarkantha, Mehsana and Himmatnagar districts, the Tribunal has evidence of the police mentioned, without naming the assailants and mob leaders whom the victim-survivors had clearly recognised during the incidents of violence.

The Commissioner of Police of Ahmedabad and Vadodara are also culpable for similar police misconduct. In far too many incidents of violence, the police refused to intervene, sided with the perpetrators of crimes, itself indulged in criminal acts, and denied curfew passes to social workers and human rights activists who, at great risk to life and limb, moved around nonetheless at the height of the violence, in a bid to restore peace. The police completely failed in providing protection to relief camps sheltering traumatised and desperate survivors, for as long as six months in many cases. Police conduct in compiling data and statistics about the loss of life, destruction of property missing persons too,has been totally callous to say the least.

One of the gravest charges made by the victim-survivors and also senior police officers too who deposed before the Tribunal, is of the great danger to the neutrality of the Gujarat police force by overt and covert measures to infiltrate it with persons owing allegiance to the thinking and mind-set of the RSS/VHP/BD and BJP.[25] The dangers of such developments cannot be over-stated. Instead of a man or a woman wedded to constitutionalism and attendant values, the result of such placements could be a police official who does not care to protect lives without fear or favour, regardless of caste, creed and community. He or she is more concerned with furthering a particular thinking that has on many an occasion in the present been the cause of the perpetration of violence.

Evidence before the Tribunal clearly indicates that since the assumption of power by the BJP in Gujarat in February 1998, there was a calculated move to sideline Muslim police officers. Muslim officers were given non-executive posts and were kept away from decision-making posts. Gujarat is the only state in the country where IPS officers who are Muslims have never been assigned the post of Deputy Superintendent of police.[26] The Tribunal is of the view that a significant section of the Gujarat police is guilty of gross dereliction of duty and of flouting the Indian Consitution and Indian criminal law. The shameful and brazenly partisan conduct of the police in the Gujarat carnage is a blot on Indian democracy and Indian secularism. Our democratic and secular crdentials are truly tested only in times of such acute crisis. In such situations, the police have been utterly partisan and communal, repeatedly failing to protect and even themselves trampling on the fundamental rights of India's religious minorities. This highly disturbing trend needs to be dealt with urgently and comprehensively.

Role of the State

Under the stewardship of Narendra Modi, Gujarat entered the second year of the 21st century on February 27, 2002 with a new kind of communal barbarism, with the chief minister and his government presiding over the well organised and systematic liquidation of the life, liberty, property, business and dignity of lakhs of Muslims across Gujarat, clearly transmitting the RSS message from Bangalore to the Muslims in Gujarat that the "Muslim minority can live in India only if they can win the goodwill of the Hindu minority" and therefore must "pay" the price for it. And what a price hundreds of innocent Muslims burnt alive, women raped, molested and killed, children and old people butchered. Even pregnant women were not spared.[27]

Thousands of houses, building and business houses with their belongings were looted and destroyed, large numbers of Muslim religious places razed to the ground and converted into Hindu temples or modern roads, more than two lakh people forced to leave their houses and to live in relief camps, without any adequate relief facilities and with no hope of just resettlement and rehabilitation,the police acting in a partisan manner, indulging in indiscriminate firings, arbitary arrests, ruthless combing, abuse of criminal process, refusal to start criminal proceedings against the criminals and closing the doors of justice on the victims.

However, the current violence tells a completely different story. The state government does not merely appear to be guilty of complacency, inefficiency or occasional connivance with the rioters. It seems to be the main sponsor of and partner in the planned massacre, loot and arson. Far from making any efforts to control the tensions generated by the Godhra carnage, the political leadership of the state went on to circulate unfounded theories of ISI-planned and financed terrorist attack on the karsevaks.

When violence started against the Muslims, it was described as a natural reaction as if to justify the same. In the evening of the February 28, after many hours of anti-Muslim violence, a senior vice president of the Vishva Hindu Parishad appeared on a news channel to justify the Bharat Bandh call for March 1st and said that the anger against the Godhra killings had not been released properly. All this explains the mood of the political leadership of the state and of the leaders of their larger parivar. Reports say the Muslims settlements were attacked by mobs that were accompanied by the police. In places where Muslim mobs resisted, the police fired on them to break their resistance. Once this was done, the attacking mobs indulged in unhindered violence of all kinds. It is also reported that ministers in the state government and senior leaders of the local BJP monitored the situation from police stations and control rooms.[28]

Gujarat 2002 looks like a glaring example of a place having what Paul Brass calls, an institutionalised riot system.[29] Gujarat having the reputation of being a Hindutva laboratory has forces that continue to stoke the communal fire, in order to keep the situation ready for a communal flare up when required. It follows from what has been mentioned earlier that this violence has seen actors who played a crucial role in converting the communal incident of Godhra into a large-scale communal flare up. It is also clear that local as well as national level sangh parivar leaders and politicians interpreted the trigger incident communally and in fact desired the violence to take place. That the leaders of the rioting mobs had detailed information about the homes and business establishments of the Muslims, that they had mobile phones to contact one another as well as their leaders, that the BJP, the VHP and the Bajrang Dal leaders were constantly monitoring the situation, all point to an informal organisational network of persons and forces, suggesting the existence of an institutionalised riot system.

In an institutionalised riot system, there are experts for playing specialised roles. During the current violence truckloads of slogan-shouters came who indulged in violence using cooking gas to set buildings ablaze. This particular riot pointed to use of cooking gas, insidious powder, etc. also required expertise.[30] Local papers like *Sandesh* and *Gujarat Samachar* excelled in rumour-mongering. Inflammatory pamphlets were circulated. It follows there were some who specialised in writing them, some others in printing them, and still others in distributing them. The performance of roles leaves scope for people for joining in without any special role assigned to them.[30]

The most important question regarding inter-religious community riots is: Can a determined state prevent such riots with an iron hand? Or, to put it differently: Can inter-religious community riots take place in a secular and religiously neutral state? The study of the relationship between the state and inter-religious community riots has assumed special significance in the context of violent riots in the state of Gujarat in 2002.[31]

Rioters are more cautious than the victims of violence and if the groups indulging in violence against a target group are unsure of support from the state apparatus and not assured a protective umbrella by state functionaries, they are likely to think twice before killing. The collusion of the state was absolute. Firstly, the state administration and the police failed to protect the lives and properties of Muslim citizens, even when several people complaining about mobs attacking their homes or shops contacted them. Many of them were told that they would have to fend for themselves on that day. Secondly, in many cases BJP, VHP and Bajrang Dal leaders including ministers and local corporators, actually led the mobs and supervised the killings and destruction.[32]

Both the state and the local media have helped the VHP and RSS in recognising the violence against the minorities. Had it not been their collusion, neither would the rioters have had such precise information about the residences and business establishments of the Muslims, nor would the RSS-VHP have been able to mobilise the enormous machinery that was developed to play havoc in Ahmedabad during this period. Thus describing the violence in Ahmedabad as a state-sponsored ethnic cleansing would appear to be appropriate.

The above description demonstrates that state power is a central issue for social scientists and social critics. Civil society or associational groups or autonomous NGOs can at best supplement the state in creating a secular society but cannot supplant it in the maintenance of social order based on respect for minorities. *Further, state and civil society are communalised if an anti-secular ideology dominant Hindu majority ideology impacts both civil society and state*. Multiculturalism, secularism, democracy, the rule of law and the principle of human equality are under attack from the forces of Hindutva.

Communalism, as historically understood, arose in the context of a colonial state required to act neutrally between conflicting communities. The state acted to restore peace without being swayed by the consideration of which community was perpetrating violence and which was targeted. In this sense, communalism was a phenomenon that essentially belonged to civil society and the state sought to control it. The Gujarat phenomenon is different because the state abandoned the time-honoured principle of even-handedness and sided with one community. Communalism relies for its operation on the creation of a mindset and control of civil society.[33]

What happened in Gujarat is a brutal manifestation of the takeover of state power by communal forces.The state allowed organised groups to go around perpetrating violence in full view of the law and order machinery. It offered justifications for that violence as if the function of the state was not to control violence but rather to adjudicate over the question of what sorts of violence it would permit and what forms it would bring under control. The principle of state neutrality in the control of communal violence was openly thrown to the wind.[34]

Understanding the Collective Violence

There are structural roots of communal violence in India; and unless far-reaching structural changes take place conflict situations will keep emerging repeatedly. Also, in the given conditions, those who hope to gain from communal polarisation and violence will continue with their game plan. The situation therefore calls for meaningful interventions by peace-loving secular and democratic forces. People's right movements involving the struggle for procedural as well as substantial democracy may provide an answer to the problem of communal violence. Participation in these movements must carve out such identities for people that may have potential to ultimately scuttle the politics of communal mobilisation. These movements may draw from different religious backgrounds. They may thus get an opportunity of obtaining a personal experience about knowledge about one another. This may serve to change the mind-set. Serious attention needs to be paid to the argument that the developmental cycle of a riot can be disturbed through outside intervention. This makes a strong case for a constant watch of the communal situation and its management by the state and the civil society. the peace-loving forces in the civil society may develop grass-root resistance to violence. They may contribute to build the bridges between communities partially isolated from each other. Finally, Gujarat is also a reminder that one of us does some introspection to find the depth and strength to our faith in secular values.

The commonly accepted picture which emerges from these writings and reports is that what we have witnessed in Gujarat are not the ordinary communal riots between Hindus and Muslims. Gujarat has had many in the past, nor are they only a part of communal divide surcharged with intense mutual hatred and hostility. We have had them in abundance in our history. What is significant and striking is that these communal disturbances commonly described as Hindu-Muslim riots, are in fact qualitatively different from earlier Hindu-Muslim riots. After Independence and particularly in 1969 and thereafter, Hindu-Muslim riots have been by and large one-sided, causing larger casualties and losers to the Muslims in general, but the present riots in Gujarat are perceived to be nothing but a kind of genocide and ethnic cleansing, comparable to what the Nazis did to the Jews in Germany.[35] These trends were visible and discernible more increasingly with each successive riot, particularly after the rise of Hindutva in the 1980s. Now they have emerged so distinctly, visibly, intensely, positively and in such an accentuated and aggravated form that the quantitative difference has become a qualitative difference, amounting to a distinct phenomenon, not of more violent and more widespread nationwide riots, but of a clear and present danger of Hindutva fascism, threatening and undermining the very basis of our constitutional system. The 'what' and 'why' of this phenomenon does not admit of any one answer or any simple explanation.[36]

All kinds of theories political, sociological, economic, cultural, historical, psychological have been propounded to explain these happenings in Gujarat, emphasising one or the other dimension of this complex phenomenon. If Gujarat is used by the Sangh Parivar as a laboratory for the Hindutva ideology, whose successful experiment can be replicated elsewhere in India, it is absolutely necessary for us to find out exactly what are the distinct elements of this successful explosion which the Hindutva forces have *ignited*. To isolate them, to understand and analyse them and to evolve proper counter strategies and an effective plan of action to deal with them is the imperative and urgent task of all of us if India is not to be what Gujarat today is. We must not allow these disruptive forces or factors or combination of forces and factors to reappear and take root elsewhere in India.[37]

The ethnic cleansing in Gujarat was a dangerous onslaught against not just one community but the whole secular and democratic ethos of the country. The result is a dangerous polarisation which goes beyond Gujarat and could take on a national character. The fact that highly educated Muslims living in cosmopolitan societies are beginning to feel that the attack is aimed at them, could well oust their confidence in pluralistic India, thereby pursuing them to a dangerous communal space. Once this happens there will be no room for genuinely secular forces who would fight and struggle for democratic and secular values and ideologies. If anything they will get pushed out of the mainstream, occupying small ideological ghettos, holding demonstrations or rallies in this city or that and at best able to find some electoral base in deep rural habitats.[38]

The communalisation and polarisation of the middle class especially the educated class is the most disturbing aspect. Once this happens, society could get polarised and come apart. At the same time the more constructive and creative polarities of class ideologies; occupations and professions are getting eroded. This is an extremely serious development, which was not there throughout the various upheavals the country has faced.

The current violence in Gujarat should be seen in the context of the total crisis sweeping through the Indian political system. The political and economic is both a cause and consequence of the processes of globalisation, authoritarianism and communalism. Globalisation has not merely opened up new economic avenues; it has also made the economic crisis worse. The political crisis emanating from inadequate responsiveness of the political system has contributed to greater authoritarian tendencies that have further distanced the people and the state, thus making the crisis even more serious. The economic and political contradictions have been manipulated to promote communalism so that it serves as an escape route for the brewing tensions.

Against this background and context, namely, communalised history, conservative and reactionary politics, social status quo, amoral, ruthless, self-centred, unjust economic growth, failure of all modernising agencies and absence of revolutionary movement, the only active, aggressive, consistent, tenacious, persistent organised, determined and fanatical group or organisation, namely, RSS and its parivar has been working with a clear political goal of pursuing and implementing the Hindutva ideology, had not faced any equally strong, persistent, tenacious, committed radical opposition either from any political party or from any people's movement and found an open field—almost a vaccum—with favourable and congenial mindset, social structure and economic ideology. And it has succeeded in creating the Gujarat of February-March 2002. The challenge is—whether we can create a strong radical people's movement committed and dedicated to socio-economic transformation both as a positive movement and as a movement against the Hindutva and secondly, whether we can influence and try to change the social, political, economic, educational, scientific, cultural spheres which can work counter to the Hindutva forces. The threat of a Hindu Rashtra is real, because unlike Islam which can provide a bulwark against amoral capitalist development, whether we like it or not, Hinduism can well accommodate and adjust amoral, unjust, ruthless capitalist consumerist development.

Intercommunal violence undermines India's stability and capacity to function as a democracy, and must be suppressed firmly. This is the first responsibility of every state and central government, and one that fails to discharge it should be required to resign as a matter of course. If need be our Constitution should be appropriately amended further and any minister or leader suspected of instigating it should be prosecuted on communal charges and disqualified from holding public office. It is scandalous that none of the political leaders implicated in any of our countless communal riots has ever been sent to prison. If we can have POTA there is no reason why we cannot enact a far more relevant prevention of an act of communal violence.[39]

The police has a crucial role to play. They should be required to act with utmost impartiality and dismissed and prosecuted for criminal negligence when shown to have failed to do so. Our criminal law needs to be revised to allow for public or private prosecution of such officers. The police act, partially because of political pressure, poor professional ethics, lack of independent control, and absence of minority officers in high positions. Determined efforts should be made to insulate them against political pressure, to improve their training, to recruit and promote qualified minority officers, and to set up independent disciplinary committees made up of the representatives of different communities and enjoying the power to conduct enquiries against partisan officers. Inter-communal violence cannot be tackled by the state alone.

The institutions of civil society have a vital role to play. It is, therefore, crucial that in all sensitive areas, extensive networks of inter-communal groups should be formed. They should be made up of the representatives of different communities with a track record of public service, interact on a regular basis with their constituents and earn their trust and good will, enjoy access to government ministers, officials and the police and be willing and able to act in times of trouble. Wherever such networks exist in the country they have played a vital role in calming passions quashing rumours providing vital intelligence and acting as a bridge between the various communities.

The real message from Gujarat is that the socio-cultural roots of Hindu communalism have not been either identified or targeted even by the secular parties and autonomous secular institutions of civil society. Gujarat has paid a very heavy price because secularists have always made tactical compromises. The Congress Party in Gujarat has to accept the responsibility for its failure to confront openly aggressively communal, social and political tendencies in the state. The conscience-keepers of Gujarati society owe an explanation to the larger Indian society for passively tolerating the growth of communalism. Riots are a consequence of the deep-seated social and historical causes, and Gujarat has once again proved this. However, the state can be pulled out of its fanatic mindset by its intellectual class, which can project an alternative secular worldview of the people there.

The attitude among the affected Mulsims in Ahmedabad today is one of sheer despondency. The myths created by the VHP-RSS regarding Muslims being heavily armed by external forces stand shattered in the face of absolutely no resistance, armed or otherwise, on the latter part. However, the fear and communal stereotypes, which have been instilled in the minds of many Hindus through years of propaganda continues to make them apprehend violent retaliation. Reports say that even trucks carrying relief material were stopped from moving into relief camps on the ground that they might be carrying arms for Muslims. It will take generations for the victims to recover from such a pointed and vicious communal onslaught. It is of immediate importance to bring the perpetrators to book and prosecute them under the criminal laws of the country.

Secular nationalism can be an effective antidote to religious fanaticism if our political processes are guided and controlled by political philosophy of secularism. Secularism essentially means prioritising citizenship over religion. Though constitutionally citizenship has priority over religion, our civil society, due to constant efforts to communalise it, is still grappling with this problem. We need committed secular citizens today for building a vibrant civil society. A vibrant civil society which is secular and democratic at heart can bring India out of communal darkness and then only a Gujarat like carnage can be prevented.

REFERENCES

1. Kamal Mitra Chenoy, et. al., "Ethno-cleansing Not Communal Riot", in Krishna Chaitanya (ed.), *Fascism in India,* Delhi: Manak Publications, 2003, p. 201.
2. Bela Bhatia, "A Step Back in Sabarkantha", in Krishna Chaitanya (ed.), op. cit., p. 301.
3. A.A. Engineer, *Communal Challenge and Secular Response*, New Delhi: Shipra Publications, 2003, p.118.
4. Kamal Mitra Chenoy, op. cit., p. 210.
5. K.N. Panikkar, "The Agony of Gujarat", *The Hindu*, March 19, 2002.
6. Pamphlet calling for economic boycott of Muslims (translated from Gujarati by NGO Sahma or see Anosh Malekar), "Silence of the Lambs." *The Week*, April 17, 2002.
7. Kunal Chattopadhyay (ed.), *The Genocidal Programme in Gujarat:*

*Anatomy of Indian Fascism,*Vadodara: Inquilabi Communist Sangathan, 2002.

8. Subhash Gatade, "Inverting Dalit Conciousness: Hindutvaising the Dalits, Communalising the Movement", in Krishna Chaitanya, op. cit., p. 340.
9. Ibid., p. 348.
10. "Genocide: Gujarat 2002", *Communalism Combat*, Mumbai, Year 8, No. 77-78, March-April, 2002.
11. V.R. Krishna Iyer, et. al., "State Complicity in Fascism in India", in Krishna Chaitanya (ed.), p. 245.
12. Ibid., p. 248.
13. Ibid., p. 260.
14. Riaz Ahmed, "Gujarat Violence: Meaning and Implications", *Economic and Political Weekly*, Vol. 37, No. 20, May 18-24, 2002, pp. 1870-1873.
15. Ibid., p. 1872.
16. V.R. Krishna Iyer, et. al., op. cit., p. 254.
17. Ibid., p. 255.
18. Ibid., p. 261.
19. Harsh Mander, "Cry, the Beloved Country: Reflections on the Gujarat Massacre", *Milli Gazette*, Delhi, April 1-15, 2002, p. 4.
20. Ibid., p. 104.
21. V.R. Krishna Iyer, et. al., op. cit., p.269.
22. A.A. Engineer, op. cit., p. 100.
23. Ibid., p. 104.
24. National Human Rights Commission Proceedings, Preliminary Commands, March 11, 2002, para X.
25. Ibid., X.
26. Ibid., para vii.
27. Bhiku Parekh, "Making Sense of Gujarat: Society Under Siege", *Seminar*, 513, May 2002, p. 26.
28. People's Union for Civil Liberties, "An Interim Report to the National Human Rights Commission", March 21, 2002.
29. Paul R. Brass, *Theft of an Idol*, Princeton: Princeton University Press, 1997, p. 127.
30. Ibid., p. 148.
31. C.P. Bhambhri, "A Society Brutalised: Is There a Way to Change People's Mindset?" in Krishna Chaitanya (ed.), op. cit., p. 575.
32. Ibid., p. 575.
33. Imtiaz Ahmad, "The State of Lies and Lies of the State", in M.L.

Sondhi and Apratim Mukharji, *The Black Book of Gujarat*, Delhi: Manak Publications, 2002.

34. Ibid., p. 383.
35. Paul R. Brass, *The Production of Hindu-Muslim Violence in Contemporary India*, Seattle: University of Washington Press, 2003, p. 383.
36. Kumaresh Chakravarty, "Towards a Genesis of the Recent Upsurge in Communalism", in Mehdi Arslan and Janaki Rajan (eds.), *Communalism in India: Challenge and Response,* New Delhi: Manohar Publications, 1994, p. 15.
37. Rajni Kothari, "Reversal of Ideology and Rise of Fascism", in Krishna Chaitanya (ed.), op. cit., p. 48.
38. Rajni Kothari, "Culture of Communalism in Gujarat", *Economic and Political Weekly*, Vol. 37, No. 48, November 30-December 6, 2002, pp. 4823-4825.
39. Bhiku Parekh in Krishna Chaitanya (ed.), op. cit., p. 519.

6

CONCLUSION

The spectre of communalism has been omnipresent in Indian political life, it is a threat to unity and to the secular ideal of the Constitution. Communalism, like linguism and regionalism is the manifestation of growing fissiparous tendencies in India. The study of communalism reveals that the problem is not purely religious or social but is largely a political and economic one. It is neither solely the product of history nor a manifestation of minority-majority consciousness but largely an outcome of the struggle between the two communities to monopolise political and economic power.

Indian communalism and communal riots have specific meaning, that is tension between Hindus and Muslims and more recently Hindu-Sikh tension has also been included under the same cover.

This study has initiated some issues relevant to Indian communalism mainly focusing on Hindu-Muslim antagonism. Slight references have been made to Hindu-Sikh communalism in order to have a comprehensive view of their communal phenomena operating in Indian social, culture, economic and political life. The debate, though old, on the close interaction between religion and politics continues to this day. Long ago Mahatma Gandhi observed that "those who say religion has nothing to do with politics do not know what religion means."

There are scholars influenced by the Gandhian approach, who have interpreted religion in the perspective of politics. Jawaharlal

Nehru departing from the Gandhian concept of combining religion with politics stressed that "religion in any real sense of the word has played little part in Indian politics." In fact the term religion is hardly used in the sense Mahatma Gandhi used it. Perhaps it was by distortion of the meaning of religion that Jawaharlal Nehru could say that religion had little to do with politics.

Communalism has been an integral part of Indian politics ever since the British introduced the principles of elected representation in public institutions. Since then religious and communal identities have been exploited and encouraged for electoral purposes. The history of the Indian National Movement unfortunately is also a history of the communalisation of Indian society. That the colonial rulers actively encouraged and aided this process is undoubtedly true, but it was essentially a result of the weakness and inadequacy of secularism as conceived and practised during the anti-colonial struggle.

In Independent India, communal politics has assumed monstrous proportions, particularly during the last twenty years. It appears to have crept into all levels of Indian polity and communal elements have acquired a substantial presence in the various apparatuses of the Indian state. A powerful influence in social consciousness has been religious identity which has given way to communitarian feeling and solidarity. Operating in this set-up, context, bourgeois politics has increasingly resorted to communalism as a positive source either for maintaining or achieving political power. In this process the relationship between politics and communalism has become complementary, the one reinforcing the other. As a result it appears that communalism would soon swamp the Indian polity.

The communal politics is essentially the manipulation of social consciousness passed on to religion for political purposes. The political parties during post-Independence India, who have tried to do so fall into two categories. First come the parties who are organised around communal ideologies, like the Hindu Mahasabha and Muslim League during the pre-Independence period and the BJP, the Akali Dal and the Muslim League in contemporary India. The parties of the second category are those parties which use communalism for political support and mobilisation without necessarily adopting communalism as the political ideology.

The contemporary communal consciousness draws upon the assumption that a distinct cultural identity exists for all those who profess the same religion. This cultural homogeneity constitutes all of them as a community within the parameters of religion. Thus Hindus, it is argued, form a single cultural community sharing the same cultural practices, distinct from the practices of Muslims or Sikhs.

The various ways adopted for communalisation by either communal parties or parties which use communitarian feeling, which could activate the two components of this dormant consciousness are religion and religious communities. The communal forces are today engaged in reinforcing and activating the religious and communitarian identities. These identities, that is a religious identity or a communitarian identity need not necessarily be communal for an identity of belonging to a religion or belonging to a community need not be against another religion or community. Yet it is important to recognise that such an identity could be transformed into communal by posing an antagonistic relationship. At a suitable social and political conjecture community consciousness could be transformed into an antagonistic communal consciousness and relationship.

Therefore, religious and communitarian identities form necessary prerequisites for communalism we are witnessing in India today cannot take place at all. There could be other forms of social strife, not communal conflict.

In the creation of communal consciousness, cultural forms and practices enter in subtle and myriad ways. The growth of print media, for instance, spawned a series of cultural productions which either induced or reflected the communal consciousness of the middle class. The innumerable pamphlets on social and religious issues, popular literature particularly on historical themes, denominational theatre staging mythological plays and so on is important in this respect.

The literature meant for children is particularly crucial as it exercises a decisive influence at the formative stage of life. There is an immense amount of communally produced children's literature, either in the form of comics or of illustrated tales. Their themes generally relate to mythology and history, with explicit religious, superstitious and communal slants. The stories from epics and religious texts are cast in an irrational and superstitious mould in order to enhance their charismatic effect and thus to appeal to young minds. The universal and secular ideas contained in religious tales are hardly emphasised.

The resurgence of communalism witnessed during the last couple of years mitigates the very foundations of Indian society, it questions the principles on which the political, social and cultural institutions and practices were nurtured during the period of the anti-colonial struggle and in post-Independence India. What is at stake is democracy, secularism, rule of law, nationalism and culture, in essence all that for what Indians fought and held dear during the last hundred years. The idea of democracy is being replaced by majoritarianism. The concept of secularism is interpreted in religious terms, the rule of law is subverted by public coercion. Indian nationalism is equated with Hindutva and Indian culture is described as Hindu culture. Thus communalism is seeking to destroy the fundamental character of Indian society, its historical legacy, cultural complexity and political institutions. This attempted subversion has led to a strong assertion by secular forces and a serious quest to find ways and means to stamp the communal tide. A necessary prerequisite for resisting communalism and for enlarging the secular space is to develop a proper understanding of the phenomenon of communalism and to make that understanding socially available.

The growing unrest is the result of the system under which the Indian government conducts domestic affairs. It is the Indian environment and short-sightedness that has created communal and short-sighted politicians.

A very powerful organising principle of present-day communalism is "correcting the mistakes committed in the past". The main burden of the argument is that temples destroyed by Muslim rulers have to be restored to the Hindus. This argument, that the temples destroyed by Muslim rulers have to be restored is based on a view that these destructions are acts of fanaticism. Thus Babri Masjid in Ayodhya or the mosques in Banaras and Mathura are viewed as symbols of Muslim "religious atrocities' on Hindus. A community-centric perspective has been developed since pre-Independence and the community syndrome has been manipulated in the post-Independence peroid. In fact after the 1980s the community-centric identity was further exploited to polarise the communities. The communal ideology has today spread its influence much beyond the middle class base. Hindu communalism is not an upper caste phenomenon any more, concerted efforts have been made by VHP and allied organisations during the NDA regime to incorporate the lower castes as well. It is indeed alarming that communalism has spread to the lower sections of the society, mainly because of the manipulation of communal forces. In this context the riots become important as a vehicle, as an instrument of communalisation. It is a very potent isstrument because once a riot takes place the division is immediately established. The nation of 'us' and 'they' which did not exist earlier is instilled into the minds of people.

A communally divided society though mainly at the level of middle classes can never become a vibrant civil society. The communal politicians are of course guilty of raising such issues and for polarising Indian society on communal lines but civil society also cannot escape its responsibility altogether. They mutually reinforce each other.

It is unfortunate that a section of educated middle class gets carried away by these sentiments and helps political parties play these games for reasons. It is for the people of India to decide which interests are dearer to them, national interests or the interests of a few religious fanatics.

It is also important to note that communalism is not only the negation of pluralism but also opposed to modernity and the concept of civil society and its political freedom. For them there is no space for modern political discourse at all. The supremacy of *dharma* is the essence of their politics. And if religion or dharma is the essence of politics non-believers can hardly have any place.

Nothing can be more valued than our diversity. Our diversity is the core of our democracy Freedom becomes meaningless without respect for this diversity. Fundamentalism and fanaticism are becoming stronger in all the countries of South Asia.

Thus the secular forces have to meet this challenge by strengthening our plurality and diversity. Polarity is the enemy of our unity. Our culture is a pluralist culture and we have deeply influenced each other in practically every field. Without shared historical bonds and sense of composite culture, sense of nationhood cannot be induced among the people. In fact citizenship is the basis of nationhood. Cultural and historical bonds are far more viable for secular politics than common religious bonds. Common religious bonds are valuable on a different plane. A religious community is different from a political community. A nation is a multi-layered community. It has several layers—political, social, historical and cultural. Despite religious differences our common cultural and historical bonds are stronger.

India's national identity needs to be so defined that all Indians, irrespective of their cultural, ethnic, religious and other differences can enthusiastically identify with it, own it with pride, and build on its basis a common sense of national belonging. It must, therefore, be defined in political terms, not cultural or religious. What all Indians share in common is their commitment to the political community of which they are all equal citizens and to which they are bound by the ties of loyalty. We need an over attacking notion, not of Hindutva but of Bharatiyata, one that affirms and cherishes our rich cultural and religious diversity and embeds it in those public values, sensibilities and institutions that we all do or should share in common.

BIBLIOGRAPHY

Primary Sources

Report of Commission of Inquiry into Ranchi and Hatia Disturbances, August 22-29, 1967, The Dayal Report, Government Central Press, Delhi, 1968.

Report of Commission of Inquiry into the Communal Disturbances at Ahmedabad and Places in Gujarat, on and after September 18, 1969, Jagmohan Reddy Report, Press Under the Department of Home Affairs.

Report of the Commission of Inquiry into the Communal Disturbances at Bhiwandi, Jalgaon, Mahad in May 1970, The Madan Commission Report, Ministry of Home Affairs, Delhi, 1975.

Report of the Commission of Inquiry into the Communal Distrubances at Bhiwandi, Ahmedabad, January-March 1984, Ministry of Home Affairs, Delhi, 1985.

Report of the Commission of Inquiry into the Delhi Riots, November 1984, Ministry of Home Affairs, Delhi, 1985.

Reports of Minority Commission, since 1960 to 1986, Ministry of Home Affairs, Delhi.

Reports of the Justice B.N. Srikrishna Commission on the Mumbai Riots of 1992-1993.

Sachchar Committee Report, Ministry of Minority Affairs, Government of India, November, 2006.

Sixth Police Commission Report, 1987, Ministry of Home Affairs, Delhi.

National Police Commission Report, 1987.

Parliamentary Debates, Since 1950-1989.

Census on Religion, 1951.

Census on Religion, 1981.

Books

Adhikari, Gangadhar M., *Resurgent India at the Cross Roads,* Bombay: People's Publishing House, 1946.

______, *Indian National Congress and Hindu-Muslim Unity,* Sydney: Current Books, 1943.

Agarwal, R.M., *Hindu-Muslim Riots: Their Causes and Cures,*Lucknow International Social Literature Publishers, 1943.

Ahmad, Imtiaz, *Family Kinship and Marriage Among Muslims in India,* New Delhi: Manohar Publications, 1976.

______, *Caste and Social Stratification Among Muslims in India,* New Delhi: Manohar Pubications, 1973.

Ahmed, Said-ud-din., *The Commercial Pattern in India*, Lahore: Ashraf Publications, 1947.

Akbar, M.J., *Riots After Riots: Reports on Caste and Communal Violence in India,* New Delhi: Penguin Books, 1988.

Akhtar, Usman, *Muslim India,* Lahore: Metropolitan Publishers, 1945.

Arslan and Rajan (ed.), *Communalism in India*: *Challenge and Response,* New Delhi: Manohar Publications, 1994.

Aziz, K.K., *Ameer Ali: Britain and Muslim India,* London: Heinemann, 1963.

Baig, M.R.A., *The Muslim Dilemma in India,* New Delhi: Vikas Publishing House, 1974.

Baird, Robert D. (ed.), *Religion in Modern India,* New Delhi: Manohar Publications, 1989.

Banu, Zenab, *Politics of Communalism: A Political-Historical Analysis of Communal Riots in Post-Independence India with Special Reference to the Gujarat and Rajasthan Riots,* Bombay: Popular Prakashan, 1989.

Barrier, N.G. (ed.), *Roots of Communal Politics,* New Delhi: Arnold-Heinemann Publishers, 1976.

Barton, William, *India's Fateful Hour,* London: John Murray 1942.

Bayley, David H., *The Police and Political Development in India,* Princeton: Princeton University Press, 1969.

Biswas, S.C. (ed.), *Gandhi: Theory and Practice; Social Impact and Contemporary Relevance*, Simla: Indian Institute of Advanced Study, 1969.

Bjorkman, J.W. (ed.), *Fundamentalism, Revivalists and Violence in South Asia,* New Delhi: Manohar Publications, 1988.

Bamford, P.C., *Histories of Non-cooperation and Khilafat Movement,* Delhi: K.K. Book Distributors, 1985.

Brass, Paul R., The Punjab Crisis and the Unity of India, In *India's Democracy: An Analysis of Exchanging State-Society Relations* edited by A. Kohli, Princeton: Princeton University Press, 1988.

______, *The Politics of India Since Independence*, Cambridge: Cambridge University Press, 1994.

______, *Theft of an Idol: Text and Context in the Representation of Collective Violence,* Princeton: Princeton University Press, 1997.

Brass, Paul R., and Robinson, Francis (eds.), *The Indian National Congress and Indian Society, 1885-1985: Ideology, Social Structure and Political Dominance,* Delhi: Chanakya Publications, 1987.

______, *Language, Religion and Politics in Northern India,* Cambridge: Cambridge University Press, 1974.

______, *The Production of Hindu-Muslim Violence in Contemporary India,* Seattle: University of Washington Press, 2003.

Broomfield, J.H., *Elite Conflict in a Plural Society,* London: Oxford University Press, 1968.

Burman, Jyotee, *Hindu-Muslim Relations: A Study of Historical Background,* Calcutta: Jagnous Sahitya Ghakra Publications, 1947.

Carras, Mary C., *Indira Gandhi; In the Crucible of Leadership: A Political Biography,* Boston: Beacon Press, 1979.

Chaitanya, Krishna (ed.), *Fascism in India; Faces, Fangs and Facts,* Manak Publications, 2003.

Chakrabarty, Bidyut (ed.), *Secularism and Indian Polity,* New Delhi: Segment Book Distributors, 1990.

Chakravarty, Kumaresh (ed.), *Communalism in India: Challenge and Response,* New Delhi: Manohar Publications, 1994,

Chand, S.M., *Communalism: Problems and Remedy,* New Delhi: National Integration Publications, 1973.

Chandra, Bipan, *Communalism in Modern India,* New Delhi: Vikas Publishing House Pvt. Ltd., 1987.

______ (ed.), *Communalism and the Writing of Indian History,* Delhi: People's Publishing House, 1969.

______, *Nationalism and Colonialism in Modern India,* Delhi: Orient Longman, 1979.

Chandra, Sudhir, *The Oppressive Present: Literature and Social Consciousness in Colonial India,* Delhi:Oxford University Press, 1992.

Chand, Tara, *History of the Freedom Movement,* New Delhi, Publications Division, 1967.

Chatterjee, Partha, *Nationalist Thought and Colonial World: A Derivative Discourse,* Delhi: Zed Books Ltd., 1986.

Chatterji, P.C., *Secular Values for Secular India,* New Delhi: Manohar Publications, 1995.

Chaudhary, Sandhya, *Gandhi and the Partition of India,* New Delhi: Sterling, 1984.

Dalwai, Hamid, *Muslim Politics in Modern India, 1857-1947,* Bombay: Nachiketa Publications, 1968.

Das, Veena (ed.), *Mirrors of Violence: Communities, Riots and Survivors in South Asia,* Delhi: Oxford University Press, 1990.

Desai, A.R., *Social Background of Indian Nationalism,* Bombay: Popular Prakashan, 1948.

Dixit, Prabha, *Communalism: A Struggle for Power,* New Delhi: Orient Longman, 1974.

Dube, S.C. and V.N. Basilov (eds.), *Secularisation in Multireligious Societies: Indo-Soviet Perspectives,* New Delhi: Concept Publishing Company, 1983.

Dumount, L., *Nationalism and Communalism in Religion, Politics and History of India, Collected Papers in Indian Sociology,* Paris: Moutan, 1970.

Dutt, R.C. (ed.), *Challenge to the Polity; Communalism, Casteism and Economic Challenges,* New Delhi: Lancer Publications, 1989.

Dutt, R.P., *India Today,* Calcutta: Manisha Publications, 1970.

Dwivedy, S. and Bharagava, G.S., *Political Corruption in India,* New Delhi: Popular Book Services, 1967.

Engineer, A.A., *Communalism and Communal Violence: An Analytical Approach to Hindu-Muslim Conflict,* Delhi: Ajanta Publications, 1989.

______ (ed.), *The Role of Minorities in the Freedom Struggle,* Delhi: Ajanta Publications, 1986.

______, *Communal Riots in Post-Independence India,* Hyderabad: Sangam Books, 1984.

______ and Shakir, Moin (eds.), *Communalism in India,* Delhi: Ajanta Publications, 1985.

______ (ed.), *Secularism and the Emerging Challenge of Communalism: Practical Aspects in the Delhi-Meerut Riots,* Delhi: Ajanta Publications, 1988.

______, *Communal Challenge and Secular Response,* New Delhi: Shipra Publications, 2003.

______, *Communalism in India: A Historical and Empirical Study,* New Delhi: Vikas Publishing House, 1996.

Esteves, Sarto, *Nationalism, Secularism and Communalism,* Delhi: South Asian Publishers, 1996.

Farooqui, M., *Indian Muslims: Problems and Trends,* Delhi: CIP, 1972.

Fernival, J.S., *Colonial Policy and Practice: A Comparative Study of Burma and Netherlands,* Cambridge: Cambridge University Press, 1948.

Frankel, Francine, *India's Political Economy 1947-2004: The Gradual Revolution,* New Delhi: Oxford University Press, 2009.

Freitag, Sandra, *Collective Action and Community: Public Arenas and the Emergence of Communalism in North India,* Berkeley: University of California, 1989.

Gajendragadkar, R.B., *Secularism and the Constitution in India,* Bombay: University of Bombay, 1971.

Geertz, C. (ed.), *Old Societies and New States: The Quest for Modernity in Asia and Africa,* Free Press of Glencoe, 1963.

Ghosh, S.K., *Communal Riots in India: Meet the Challenge Unitedly,* New Delhi: Ashish Publishing House, 1987.

Ghurye, G.S., *Social Tensions in India,* Bombay: Popular Prakashan, 1968.

Gopal, Sarvepalli (ed.), *Anatomy of a Confrontation: The Babri Masjid-Ramjanmabhumi Issue*, New Delhi: Penguin Books, 1991.

Gauba, K.L., *Passive Voices: A Penetrating Study of Muslims in India,* New Delhi: Sterling Publishers, 1973.

Hamid, Abdul, *Muslim Separatism in India: A Brief Survey, 1858-1947,* London: Oxford University Press, 1967.

Hardy, P., *The Muslims of British India,* Cambridge: Cambridge University Press, 1972.

Harman, S., *Plight of Muslims in India,* London: D.L. Publications 1977.

Hart, Henry (ed.), *Indira Gandhi's India: A Political System Reappraised,* Boulder: West View Press, 1976.

Hasan, Mushirul, *Communal and Pan-Islamic Trends in Colonial India,* New Delhi: Manohar Publications, 1985.

______, *Nationalism and Communal Politics in India 1885-1930,* New Delhi: Manohar Publications, 1991.

______, (ed.), *The Unfinished Agenda: Nation Building in South Asia,* New Delhi: Manohar Publications, 2001.

______, *India Partitioned: The Other Face of Freedom,* 2 vols., New Delhi: Roli Books, 1997.

Hasan, Zoya, et.al., *The State, Political Process and Identity: Reflection of Modern India,* New Delhi: Sage Publications, 1989.

Haq, Mushirul, *Islam in Secular India,* Simla: Indian Institute of Advanced Study, 1972.

______, *Muslim Politics in Modern India, 1857-1947,* Meerut: Meenakshi Prakashan, 1970.

Horowitz, L. Donald, *The Deadly Ethnic Riot,* University of California Press, 2002.

Hunter, W.W., *The Indian Muslims,* Delhi: Indological Book House, 1969.

Hussain, S. Abid, *The Destiny of Indian Muslims,* New York: Asia Publishing House, 1965.

Irene, Tinker and Park L. Richards, (eds.), *Leadership and Political Institutions in India,* Greenwood Press,1969.

Imam, Zaffar (ed.), *Muslims in India,* Delhi: Orient Longman, 1975.

Jaffery, Robin, *What's Happening to India? Punjab Ethnic Conflict and the Test for Federalism,* Hong Kong: Macmillan, 1986

Kabir, Humayun, *Minorities in a Democracy,* Calcutta: Firma K.L. Mukhopadhyay Pvt. Ltd., 1968

Kakkar, Sudhir, *The Inner World: Psychoanalytic Study of Childhood and Society in India,* New Delhi: Oxford University Press, 1978.

Kapur, Rajiv, *Sikh Separatism: The Politics of Faith,* London: Allen and Unwin, 1986.

Karunakaran, K.P., *Religion and Political Awakening in India,* Meerut: Meenakshi Prakashan, 1965.

Kashyap, Anirban, *Communalism and Constitution,* New Delhi: Lancers, 1988.

Kaul, Jolly Mohan, *Problems of National Integration,* New Delhi: People's Publishing House, 1963.

Kaur, Amarjit, et. al. (ed.), *The Punjab Story,* New Delhi: Roli Books, 1984.

Kaura, Uma, *Muslims and Indian Nationalism: The Emergence of the Demand for India's Partition, 1928-40,* New Delhi: Manohar Publications, 1977.

Keswani, K.B., *History of Modern India, 1819-1964,* Bombay: Himalaya Publishing House, 1990.

Khan, Abdul Majid, *The Communalism in India: Its Origin and Growth,* Lahore: Paramount Publications, 1944.

Kohli, Atul, *Democracy and Discontent: India's Growing Crisis of Governability,* Cambridge: Cambridge University Press, 1990

______ (ed.), *India's Democracy: An Analysis of Changing State and Society Relations,* Princeton: Princeton University Press, 1988.

______, *The State and Poverty in India: The Politics of Reform,* Cambridge: Cambridge University Press, 1987.

Kochanek, Stanley, *Business and Politics in India,* Berkeley: University of California Press, 1974.

Kosambi, D.D., *Myth and Reality: Studies in the Formation of Indian Culture,* Bombay: Popular Prakashan, 1962.

Kothari, Rajni, *Politics in India,* Delhi: Orient Longman, 1982.

______, *State Against Democracy: In Search of Humane Governance,* Delhi: Ajanta Publications, 1988.

______, *Democratic Polity and Social Change in India: Crisis and Opportunities,* Bombay: Allied Publishers, 1976.

______, *Politics and The People: In Search of a Humane India,* Delhi: Ajanta Publications, 1989.

______, *Communalism in Indian Politics,* Ahmedabad, Rainbow Publications, 1998.

Krishna, K.B., *The Problem of Minorities or Communal Representation in India,* London: George Allen and Unwin Ltd., 1939.

Kulkarni, V.B., *India and Pakistan: A Historical Survey of Hindu-Muslim Relations*, Bombay: Jaico Publishing House, 1973.

Kumar, Anand, *State and Society in India: A Study of the State's Agenda-Making, 1917-1977,* Delhi: Radiant Publishers, 1989.

Kumar, Pramod, *Polluting Sacred Faith: A Study of Communalism and Violence in India*, Delhi: Ajanta Publications,1992

Kumar, Ravinder, *Essays in the Social History of Modern India,* New Delhi: Oxford University Press, 1983.

Kumar, Ravindra, *Problem of Communalism in India,* Delhi: Mittal Publications, 1990.

Lal, Ramji, *Political India: 1935-42; Anatomy of Indian Politics,* Delhi: Ajanta Publications, 1986.

______ (ed), *The Communal Problem in India: A Symposium,* Karnal: Dayal Singh College Publications, 1988.

Lapence, S.A., *The Protection of Minorities,* New York:UN, 1967.

Lele, Jayant K. and Rajendra Vora (eds.), *Boeings and Bullock Carts: State and Society in India,* Delhi: Chanakya Publications, 1990.

Lohia, Ram Manhor, *Guilty Men of India's Partition,* Hyderabad: Ram Manohar Lohia Samata Vidyalaya Nyas Publication, 1970.

Loomis, Charles P. and Zonak Loomis, *Socio-Economic Change and Religious Factor in India: An Indian Symposium of Views on Max Weber,* Affiliated East-West Press, 1969.

Lyon and Manor (eds.), *Transfer and Transformation of Political Institutions in the New Commonwealth,* New Hampshire: Leicester University Press, 1983.

Madan, T.N. (ed.), *Religion in India,* Delhi: Oxford University Press, 1992.

Madhok, Balraj, *Indianisation: What, Why and How?,* New Delhi: S. Chand & Co., 1970.

Mehta, Dharam Veer, *Sociology of Communal Violence*, New Delhi: Anmol Publications,1998.

Malkani, K.R., *The Midnight Knock,* New Delhi: Vikas Publishing House, 1978.

Mammen, P.M., *Communalism Versus Communalism: A Study of the Socio-Religions Communities and Political Parties in Kerala, 1892-1970,* Calcutta: Minerva Publications, 1981.

Manor, James, *Political Change in Indian States, Mysore 1917-1955,* New Delhi: Manohar Publications, 1978.

Marx, Karl and F. Engels, *Pre-Capitalist Socio-Economic Formation: A Collections,* Moscow: Progress Publishers.

Mathur, Y.B., *Muslims in Changing India,* Delhi: Trimurti Publications, 1972.

Mohan, Radhey, *Secularism in India: A Challenge,* Delhi: Dr. Zakir Husain Educational and Cultural Foundation Publications, 1990.

Moraes, Frank, *India Today,* New York: Macmillan, *1960.*

Mujeeb, M., *The Indian Muslims,* London: George Allen and Unwin, 1967.

Murphy, Gordner, *In the Minds of Men: The Study of Human Behaviour and Social Tensions in India,* New York: Basic Books, 1955.

Naidu, R., *Communal Edge to Plural Society: India and Malaysia,* New Delhi: Vikas Publishing House 1980.

Narang, A.S., *Storm Over the Sutlej: The Akali Politics,* New Delhi: Gitanjali Publishing House 1983.

Nayar, Baldev Raj, *Violence and Crime in India: A Quantitative Study,* New Delhi: Macmillan, 1975.

Nayak, Pradeep, *Politics of Ayodhya Dispute: Rise of Communalism and Future Voting Behaviour,* New Delhi: Commonwealth Publishers, 1993.

Nathan, Glazer and P. Daniel Moynihan: *Beyond the Melting Pot: The Negroes, Puerto Ricans, Jews, Italians and Irish of New York City,* USA: M.I.T. Press, 1973.

Nehru, Jawaharlal, *Selected Works of Jawaharlal Nehru,* Vol. VI, New Delhi: Orient Longman,1972.

Pande, B.N. (ed.), *National Intergration,* Bombay: Popular Prakashan, 1970.

Pandey, Gyanendra, *The Construction of Communalism in Colonial North India,* New Delhi: Oxford University Press, 1990.

Panikkar, K.N. (ed.), *Communalism in India: History, Politics and Culture*, Delhi: Manohar Publications, 1990.

Patwardhan, M.V., *Nehru-Tandon Reconciled or the Solution of the Communal Problem,* M.V. Patwardhan, original from the University of California,1952.

Phillips, C.E. and M.D. Wainright, *The Partition of India: Policies and Perspectives,1935-1947,* London: Allen and Unwin Ltd., 1970.

Pirzada, S.S. (ed.), *Foundation of Pakistan,* Karachi: Metropolitan Publishers, 1969.

Prasad, Beni, *India's Hindu-Muslim Question,* London: George Allen and Unwin Ltd., 1946.

Prasad, I., and Subedar, *Hindu-Muslim Problem,* Allahabad: Chugh Publications, 1974.

Robinson, Francis, *Separatism Among Indian Muslims: The Politics of the United Provinces' Muslims, 1860-1923,* London: Cambridge University Press, 1974.

Rajgopal, D.R., *Communal Violence in India,* New Delhi: Uppal Publishing House, 1987.

Rao, R.V.R. (ed.), *Indian Unity: A Symposium,* Delhi: Publications Division, Ministry of Information & Broadcasting, Government of India, 1969.

Rudolph, L. Lloyd and Susanne Hoeber Rudolph, *In Pursuit of Lakshmi: The Political Economy of the Indian State,* Bombay: Orient Longman, 1987.

Rudolph, L.I. (ed.), *Cultural Policy in India,* Delhi: Chanakya Publications, 1984.

Saberwal, Satish, *India: The Roots of Crisis,* Delhi: Oxford University Press, 1986.

Saksena, N.S., *Communal Riots in India,* Noida: Trishul Publications, 1990.

Sankhdhar, M.M., *Reflections on Indian Politics*, New Delhi: Kumar Brothers, 1973.

Sankhdhar, M.M. and K.K. Wadhwa (eds.), *National Unity and Religious Minorities,* New Delhi: Gitanjali Publishing House, 1991.

Schermnhorn, R.A., *Ethnic Plurality in India,* Tucson: University of Arizona Press, 1978.

Schuster, George and Guy Wint, *India and Democracy,* Biblio Bazaar, 2011.

Sarkar, Sumit, *Modern India 1885-1947,* Bombay: Macmillan India Ltd., 1983.

Shah, A.B. (ed.), *Challenges to Secularism,* Bombay: Nachiketa Publications, 1968.

Shah, A.B., *Religion and Society in India,* Bombay: Somaiya Publications, 1981.

Shakir, Moin (ed.), *State and Politics in Contemporary India,* Delhi: Ajanta Publications, 1989.

______, *Muslims in Free India,* New Delhi: Kalamkar Prakashan, 1972.

Sharma, Asha, *Socio-Economic Roots of Communalism*, J.N.U., unpublished M. Phil. Dissertation, 1984.

Sharma, G.S. (ed.), *Secularism: Its Impication for Law and Life in India,* New Delhi: The Indian Law Institute, 1966.

Sharma, Sita Ram, *Anatomy on Communalism: Historical Perspectives on Communalism,* New Delhi: APH Publications, 1998.

Shukla, K.S. (ed.), *Collective Violence: Genesis and Responses,* New Delhi: Indian Institute of Public Administration, 1988.

Singh, Amrik (ed.), *Punjab in Indian Politics: Issues and Trends,* Delhi: Ajanta Publications, 1985.

Singh, Dalip, *Dynamics of Punjab Politics,* New Delhi: Macmillan, 1981.

Singh, Khushwant, *A History of the Sikhs,* Vol. II, New Delhi: Oxford University Press, 1966.

______ and Bipan Chandra, *Many Faces of Communalism,* Chandigarh: Centre for Research in Rural and Industrial Development, 1985.

Singh, Mohinder, *The Akali Movement,* New Delhi: Macmillan, 1978.

Sinha, V.K. (ed.), *Secularism in India,* Bombay, Lalvani Publishing House, 1968.

Siwach, J.R., *Dynamics of Indian Government and Politics,* New Delhi: Sterling Publishers Pvt. Ltd., 1985.

Smith, D.E., *India As A Secular State,* UMI books on demand,1993.

Smith, Wilfred Cantwell, *Modern Islam in India: A Social Analysis,* New Delhi: Usha Publicaitons, 1979.

Sondhi, M.L. (ed), *The Black Book of Gujarat,* Delhi: Manak Publications, 2002.

Srinivas, M.N., *Social Change in Modern India,* Bombay: Allied Publishers, 1966.

S. Navlakha (ed.), *Studies in Asian Social Development,* New Delhi: Vikas Publishing House, 1974.

Thapar, Romila, et.al., *Communalism and the Writing of Indian History,* New Delhi: People's Publishing House, 1969.

Tully, Mark and Satish Jacob, *Amritsar: Mrs. Gandhi's Last Battle,* London: Jonathan Cape, 1985.

Usman, Akhtar, *Muslim India,* Lahore: Paramount Publications, 1945.

Vanaik, Achin, *The Painful Transition: Bourgeois Democracy in India,*

London: Verso Books, 1990.

______, *Communalism Contested: Religion, Modernity and Secularisation,* New Delhi: Vistaar Publications, 1997.

Varshney, Ashutosh, *Ethnic Conflict and Civil Society: India and Beyond,* Massachusetts Institute of Technology, 2000.

Verma, S.L., *On Grounds of Gandhian Polity: Leadership, Relevance and Problems,* Jaipur: RBSA Publishers, 1990.

Weiner, Myron, *Party Building in a New Nation: The Indian National Congress,* Chicago: University of Chicago Press, 1967.

Wilcox, Wayne, *Political Modernisation in South Asia,* California Rand Corporation, 1968.

Zakaria, Rafiq, *Rise of Muslims in Indian Politics: An Analysis of Developments from 1985 to 1906,* Bombay: Somaiya Publications, 1970.

Zine, Max Jean, *Strains on Indian Democracy: Reflections on India's Political and Institutional Crisis,* New Delhi: ABC Publishing House, 1988.

Articles

Aggarwal, P.C., "Islamic Revival in Modern India: The Case of the Meus", *Economic and Political Weekly,* Vol. 4, No. 2, October 18, 1969, pp. 1677, 1679-1681.

Ahmad, Imtiaz, "Communal Riots in India", *The Times of India,* December 1, 1987.

______, "Secularism and Communalism", *Economic and Political Weekly,* Vol. 4, July 28-29, 1969, pp. 1137-1152.

_______, "Political Economy of Communalism in Contemporary India", *Economic and Political Weekly,* Vol. 19, No. 22/23, June 2-9, 1984, pp. 903-906.

______, "Perspective of Communal Problem", *ICSSR Quarterly* 11, 1972.

______, "Indian Muslims and Electoral Politics", *Economic and Political Weekly,* Vol. 2 , No. 19, March 11, 1967.

Ahmed, Riaz, "Gujarat Violence: Meaning and Implications", *Economic and Political Weekly,* Vol. 37, No. 20, May 18-24, 2002, pp. 1870-1873.

Asaf Ali, Aruna, "Reminiscing Over Three Decades and More." *Link,* Vol. 34, No.1, August 18, 1991.

Baird, Robert, "Religion and the Secular: Categories for Religious Conflict and Religious Change in Independent India", *Journal of Asian and African Studies,* Vol. 11, Nos. 1-2, January 1976, pp. 47-63.

Banerjee, Sumanta, "Militancy, Violence and Democratic Rights", *Philosophy and Social Action,* Vol. 16, No. 2, April-June 1990, pp. 51-56.

Bayely, David H., "The Police and Political Order in India", *Asian Survey,* Vol. 23, No. 4 , April 1983, pp. 848-96.

Bhardwaj, Krishna.,"Economic Development and Communalism: A Note", *Social Scientist* 18, Nos. 8-9, August-September 1990.

Brass, Paul R., "Review: Class, Ethnic Group and Party in Indian Politics", *World Politics,* Vol. 33, No. 3, April 1981, p. 453.

Bryjak, George, "Collective Violence in India," *Asian Affairs,* Vol. 13, No. 2, Summer 1986, pp. 35-53.

Chakravarthy, Nikhil, "Congress (I) and Communalism", *Deccan Herald,* Bangalore, November 14, 1989.

Chakravarty, Sukhmoy, "India's Development Strategy for the 1980s", *Economic and Political Weekly,* Vol. 19, Nos. 20-21, May 26, 1984, pp. 845-52.

Chand, Tara, "Historical Origins of Communal Problem", *Secular Democracy*, Annual Number, 1974.

Chandra, Bipan, "Communalism in Retrospect", *Mainstream,* Vol. xxi, No. 45, July 9, 1983, pp. 8-15.

______, "Communalism–The Way Out-1", *The Hindustan Times*, June 1, 1987.

______, "Politics of Communalism", *Third Concept,* Vol. 4, Nos. 50-51, April-May 1991, pp. 21-22

______, "Communalism and the State: Some Issues in India", *Social Scientist,* Vol. 18, No. 8-9, August-September 1990, pp. 39-47.

Charu and Mukul, "Hindi Language Press and Bhagalpur Riots", *Mainstream,* Vol. 28, No. 20, March 10, 1990, pp. 18-20.

______, "Communal Riots and the Media", *Hindustan Times,* May 22, 1989.

______, "Secular Outlook" *India International Centre Quarterly,* Vol. 14, No. 4, Winter 1987, pp. 25-30.

Chaubey, N.P., "Role of Mass Communication in Fostering National Integration", *Bhartiya Samajik Chintan*, Vol. 7, Nos. 3-4, September-December 1987, pp. 50-63.

Choudhary, Mrinal Dutta, "The New Policy", *Seminar,* December 1985, pp. 18-22.

Chawla, N.C., "Mass Media and National Integration", *Mainstream,* Vol. 22, No. 22, Republic Day 1984, pp. 15-67.

Chibber, Pradeep K. and Petrocik Johr, "Puzzle of Indian Politics: Social

Cleavages and the Indian Party System", *British Journal of Political Science,* Vol. 19, No. 2, April 1989, pp. 191-210.

______, "Communalism and History Linking the Unlinkable", *Frontiers,* Vol. 23, No. 28, February 23, 1991.

Das, Suranjan, "Communal Violence in Twentieth Century Colonial Bengal: An Anlytical Framework", *Social Scientist,* Vol. 18, Nos. 6-7, June–July 1990.

Datta, Pradip, et. al., "Understanding Communal Violence: Nizamuddin Riots," *Economic and Political Weekly,* Vol. 25, No. 45, November 10, 1990.

Datta, Bhabatosh, "The Road to Nowhere", *Seminar 316,* December 1985, pp. 32-35.

D'Cruz, Emil, "Indian Secularism and Communalism: A Theoretical Framework", *Social Action,* Vol. 37, No. 3, July-September 1987, pp. 213-27.

Deitrich, Gabriel, "Crisis of Culture and Upsurge of Communalism in India?" *Marxist Review,* Vol. 13, No. 3, September 1979, pp. 213-27.

Deshingkar, G. and R. Kothari, "Punjab the Longer View." *Illustrated Weekly of India,* July 15, 1984, pp. 20-23.

Dhillon, Satwinder Singh, "Evolution of the Sikh Community", *New Quest,* No. 77, September-October 1989, pp. 275-86.

Dilip, Simeon "Communalism in Modern India", *Social Scientist Probings,* Vol. 9, No. 1 (March 1987), pp. 47-71.

Dogra, Bharat, "Challenge of Seccessionism and Communalism", *Mainstream,* Vol. 29, No. 7, December 8, 1990, pp. 26-27.

D'Souza, Victor S., "Roots of Present Communal Crisis", *Economic and Political Weekly,* Vol. 26, No. 21, May 25, 1991, pp. 1333-1335.

Dumont, Louis, "Nationalism and Communalism", *Contributions to Indian Sociology,* Vol. 7, 1964, p. 50.

Engineer, A.A., "Grim Tragedy of Bhagalpur Riots: Role of Police-Criminal Nexus", *Economic and Political Weekly,* Vol. 25, No. 6, February 10, 1990, pp. 305-307.

______, "Communalism: Its Theoretical and Practical Dimensions", *Islamic Perspective,* Vol. 3, No. 3, July 1987.

______, "Communalism, Communal Violence and Human Rights," *India International Centre,* Vol. 13, No. 3-4, December 1986, pp. 161-72.

______, "Communal Riots in Recent Months", *Economic and Political Weekly,* Vol. 25, No. 40, October 6, 1990, pp. 2234-36.

______, "Lok Sabha Elections and Communalisation of Politics", *Economic and Political Weekly,* Vol. 26, No. 27-28, July 6, 1991, pp. 1649-52.

______, "Towards a Materialist Explanation of Communal Violence", *South Asia Bulletin,* Vol. 7, Nos. 1-2, January 1987, pp. 50-55.

______, "From Caste to Communal Violence", *Economic and Political Weekly,* Vol. 20, No. 15, April 13, 1985, pp. 628-30.

______, "Socio-Economic Basis of Communalism", *Mainstream,* Vol. 21, No. 45, July 9, 1983, pp. 15-18.

______, "Politician and Communal Violence", *The Hindustan Times*, November 6, 1989.

Evans, Peter, "Predatory Developmental and Other Apparatuses: A Comparative Political Economy Perspective on the Third World State", *Sociological Forum,* Vol. 4, No. 4, 1989, pp. 561-87.

Gangwal, Sumit, "Communalism and Political Process", *Political Science Review,* Vol. 27, Nos. 1-4, January-December 1988.

George, Alex, "Sultan and the Saffron", *Economic and Political Weekly,* Vol. 25, No. 52, December 29, 1990.

Gill, S.S and K.C. Singhal, "The Punjab Problem: Its Historical Roots", *Economic and Political Weekly,* Vol. 19, No. 14, April 1984, p. 604.

Girdner, Eddle J., "Social Ferment in India", *Bulletin of Concerned Asian Scholars,* Vol. 19, No. 3, July-August 1987, p. 57

Gopal, S., "Nation Building, Development Process and Communication: A Historical Perspective of Communalism in India." *Third Concepts,* Vol. 4, Nos. 50-51, April-May, 1991, pp. 34-36.

Goyal, D.R., "Heroes of Our Time", *National Herald,* October 13, 1990.

______, "Nexus Between Politics and Violence," *National Herald,* March 9, 1991.

Grewal, O.P. and K.L. Tuteja, "Communalism and Fundamentalism: A Dangerous Form of Anti-Democratic Politics", *Economic and Political Weekly,* Vol. 25, No. 47, November 24, 1990, pp. 2592-2593.

Gupta, Dipankar, "Communalism and Fundamentalism: Some Notes on the Nature of Ethnic Politics in India", *Economic and Political Weekly,* Vol. 26, Nos. 11-12, Annual 1991, pp. 573-582.

Gupta, Rakesh, "Indian Interpretations of Communalism", *Man and Development,* Vol. 10, No. 1, March 1988, pp. 96-112.

Habib, Irfan., "Problems of the Muslim Minority in India", *Social Scientist,* Vol. 4, No. 11, June 1976, pp. 67-72.

Hasan, Mushirul, "Religion and Politics: The Ulama and the Khilafat Movement", *Economic and Political Weekly,* Vol. 16, No. 2, May 16, 1981, pp. 903-912.

______, "Communal and Revivalist Trends in Congress", *Social Scientist,* Vol. 8, No. 7, February 1980, p. 55.

Hasan, Zoya, "Changing Orientation of the State and the Emergence of Majoritarianism in the 1980s", *Social Scientist,* Vol. 18, Nos. 8-9, August-September 1990, pp. 135-38.

______, "Minority Identity, Muslim Women's Bill Campaign and the Political Process", *Economic and Political Weekly,* Vol. 24, No. 1, January 7, 1989, pp. 44-50.

Husain, Moinrul, Muslim Question in India, *Journal of Contemporary Asia,* Vol. 19, No. 3, 1989.

Hazari, R.K., "Communalism: Perception and Counter Perceptions", *Mainstream,* Vol. 24, No. 48, August 2, 1986, pp. 7-9.

Jain C.M. and C.L. Sharma, "Communal Economy and the Problems of Governmental Control", *The Indian Political Science Review,* Department of Political Science, University of Delhi, Vol. 5, No. 2, April-September 1971, p. 128.

Jain, Girilal, "Discussion: The Past and the Future," *Mainstream,* Vol. 29, No. 42, August 10, 1991.

______, "The Communal Problem", *The Times of India,* October 16, 1974, p. 6.

Johnson, Gordon, "Indian Independence: Taking the Strain, Cutting the Knot", *Asian Affairs,* Vol. 16, No. 3, October 1985, pp. 254-64.

Joshi, K.K., "Genesis of Communal Discord", *The Tribune,* Chandigarh, August 27, 1987.

Joshi P.C., "Secularism and the Religiosity of the Oppressed: Some Reflections", *Man and Development,* Vol. 9, No. 4, December 1987, pp. 201-37.

Joshi, Sashi, "Communalism and Role of Ideology." *The Patriot,* December 5, 1984.

Kanjilal, Partik, "Bhagalpur: The Scars that Remain", *The Statesman,* October 27, 1990.

Kaviraj, Sudipta, "On the Crisis of Political Institutions in India", *Contributions to Indian Sociology,* Vol. 18, No. 2, November 1984, pp. 223-44.

______, "Indira Gandhi and Indian Politics", *Economic and Political Weekly,* Vol. 21, No. 38/39, September 20-27, 1986, pp. 1697-1708.

Kesselman, Amrita and Mark Kesselman, "Class, Communalism and Official Complicity: India after Indira", *Monthly Review,* Vol. 36, No. 8, January 1985, pp. 13-21.

Khan, Rasheeduddin, "Understanding India's Communal Politics",

Mainstream, Vol. 7, No. 26, March 1, 1969, pp. 10-11.

______, "Nation Building Process in South Asia and the Phenomenon of Communalism", *Contemporary Affairs,* Vol. 2, No. 2, April-June 1988, pp. 3-19.

______, "Challenge of Communalism", *World Focus 8,* Nos. 11-12, November-December 1987: 3-6.

Khan, Arshi, "Dragons's Teeth of BJP", *Mainstream,* Vol. 29, No. 25, April 13, 1991.

Kohli, Atul, "Politics of Economic Liberalisation in India", *World Development,* Vol. 17, Issue No. 3, 1989, pp. 305-328.

Kothari, Rajni, "New Frontier of Politics", *Radical Humanists,* Vol. 54, No. 1, April 1990.

______, "Culture of Communalism in Gujarat", *Economic and Political Weekly,* Vol. 37, No. 48, November 30-December 6, 2002, pp. 4823-4825.

______, "Integration and Exclusion in Indian Politics", *Economic and Political Weekly,* Vol. 23, No. 43, October 22, 1988, pp. 2223-28.

______, "The Congress System in India", *Asian Survey,* Vol. 4, No. 12, December 1964, pp. 1161-73.

______, "The Great Divide", *Illustrated Weekly,* September 1985.

______, "Communalism in India: The New Face of Democracy", *Lokayan Bulletin,* New Delhi, June 3, 1985, p. 56.

______, "Cultural Context of Communalism", *Radical Humanist,* Vol. 54, No. 1, April 1990, p. 42.

Krishna, Gopal, "Indian Muslims and Electoral Politics", *Economic and Political Weekly,* Vol. 2, No. 10, March 11, 1967, pp. 187-192.

______, "Communal Issue Revisited", *The Times of India,* October 10, 1974.

______, "Communal Violence in India: A Study of Communal Disturbance in Delhi", *Economic and Political Weekly,* Vol. 20, No. 2, January 12, 1985, pp. 61-74.

Kumar, Pradeep, "Communal Dimension of Regionalism in Indian, Federation: A Study of Trends in Akali Politics, *Indian Journal of Politics,* Vol. 13, No.1/2, April-August 1979, pp. 108-116.

______, "Problems of National Integration: A Study of Communal Violence in India Since Independence", *Indian Journal of Political Science,* Vol. 18, No. 2, June 1984, pp. 115-120.

Kumar, Pramod, "Communalism in India: Some Theoretical Issues", *Man and Development,* Vol. 8, No. 4, December 1986, pp. 35-62.

Madan, T.N., "Secularism in its Place", *Journal of Asian Studies,* Vol. 46, No. 4, November 1987, pp. 747-759.

Malekar, Anosh "Silence of the Lambs", *The Week*, April 17, 2002.

Malik, Y.K. and D.K. Vajpeyi, "Rise of Hindu Militancy: India's Secular Democracy at Risk", *Asian Survey,* Vol. 29, No. 3, March 1989, pp. 308-325.

Malkani, K.R., "Some BJP Thoughts for the Left", *Mainstream,* Vol. 28, No. 39, July 21, 1990.

______, "Justice for All and Appeasement of None: Concepts of Nationalism versus Communalism in Historical Perspective", *Manthan*, Vol. 10, No. 10, September 1989.

______, "A Cry from the Head", *The Hindu,* Madras, November 14, 1990.

Mander, Harsh, "Cry, the Beloved Country: Reflections on the Gujarat Massacre", *Milli Gazette,* Delhi, April 1-15, 2002, p. 4.

Manor, James, "How and Why Liberal and Representative Politics Emerged in India", *Political Studies,* Vol. 38, Issue 1, March 1990, pp. 20-38.

______, "Collective Conflict in India", *Conflict Studies,* 1988.

Mathews, Jim, "Indian Politics Since 1947: A Historical Overview", *World Review,* Vol. 22, No. 4, October 1983, pp. 5-26.

Mathur, G.B. and S. Sahay, "Hindu Fundamentalism and Minority Alienation in India", *New Quest* 74, March-April 1989, pp. 69-75.

Mathur, Virish, "Eliminate Anti Confessions from Political Life," *Links,* Vol. 33, No. 21, December 30, 1990.

Melson, Robert and Howard Wolpe, "Modernisation and the Politics of Communalism: A Theoretical Perspective", *American Political Science Review,* Vol. 64, No. 4, December 1970, pp. 116-130.

Mishra, S.C. "Over Secrecy in Reporting Communal Incidents", *Indian Journal of Public Administration,* Vol. 25, No. 4, October-December 1979, pp. 1207-1213.

Mohan, Surendra "Politics of Communalism", *Third Concepts,* Vol. 4, Nos. 50-51, April-May 1991, pp. 6-9.

Mukherjee, Nirmal, "Communal Divide: Who Will Guard the Guards?", *Seminar* 374, October 1990, pp. 14-17.

Mukhia, Harbans, "Communalism and Indian Politics", *Economic and Political Weekly,* Vol. 18, No. 39, September 24, 1983, p. 1664.

Namboodiripad, E.M.S. "Reassertion of Faith", *Man and Development,* Vol. 12, No. 4, December 1990.

______, "National Unity and Communal Amity", *Patriot,* December 12, 1990.

Nandy, Ashis, "Politics of Secularism and the Recovery of Religious Tolerance", *Alternatives,* Vol. 13, No. 2, April 1990, pp. 177-94.

______, "An Anti-Secularist Manifesto", *Seminar* 314, October 1985, pp. 14-24.

Nayak, Pradeep, "Congress Party and Political Stability", *Mainstream,* Vol. 29, No. 29, May 11, 1991, p. 14-16.

Noorani, A.G., "The Grievances of Indian Muslims", *Secular Democracy,* August 1969, p. 3.

______, "BJP's Assault on Minoritism: Lesson from Britain", *Economic and Political Weekly,* Vol. 25, No. 33, August 18, 1990.

Owen, F. Hugh, "Negotiating the Lucknow Pact", *Journal of Asian Studies,* Vol. 31, No. 3, May 1972, pp. 561-587.

Pandey, Gyanendra, "Questions of Nationalism and Communalism", *Economic and Political Weekly,* Vol. 22, No. 25, June 20, 1987, pp. 983-984.

______, "In Defence of the Fragment: Writing About Hindu-Muslim Riots in India Today", *Representations,* No. 37, 1992: 27.

Panikkar, K.N., "The Agony of Gujarat", *The Hindu,* March 19, 2002.

Parekh, Bhiku, "Making Sense of Gujarat: Society Under Siege", *Seminar* 513, May 2002, p. 26.

Patel, Sujata, "Collapse of Government", *Economic and Political Weekly,* Vol. 20, No. 16, April 27, 1985, pp. 749-750.

______, "Debacle of Populist Politics", *Economic and Political Weekly,* Vol. 20, No. 16, April 20, 1985, pp. 681-682.

Punjabi, Riyaz, "Inter Religious Conflicts and Rise of Fundamentalism in India", *Mainstream,* Vol. 29, No. 11, January 5, 1991, pp. 15-21.

Puri, Harish K., "The Akali Agitation: An Analysis of Socio-Economic Basis of Protest", *Economic and Political Weekly,* Vol. 18, No. 4, January 22, 1983. p. 115.

Puri, Yogesh, "Reexamining Religion, Communalism and Communal Riots", *Mainstream,* Vol. 29, No. 23, March 23, 1991.

Rajagopal, P.R., "How Violence Has Grown", *The Hindustan Times,* August 21, 1987, p. 9.

Ray, Ashwani, "Communal Politics and Communal Violence", *Mainstream,* September 1981, p. 53.

Roy, Shantimoy, "Bhagalpur Carnage in Perspective", *Mainstream* 28, No. 20, March 10, 1990, pp. 15-17, 28.

Roy, Asim, "High Politics of India's Partition: The Revisionist Perspective", *Modern Asian Studies,* Vol. 24, No. 2, May 1990.

Rudolph Lloyd and Susan Rudolph, "Transformation of Congress Party: Why 1980 Was Not Restoration", *Economic and Political Weekly,* Vol. 16, No. 18, May 2, 1981, 811, 813, 815, 818.

Saberwal, Satish, "Modelling the Crisis: Mega Society, Multiple Codes and Social Blanks", *Economic and Political Weekly,* Vol. 20, No. 5, February 2, 1985, 202-11.

Sainath, P., "Press and Communalism", *Social Scientist,* Vol. 18, March 1990, pp. 158-160.

Sarkar, Chanchal, 'Communal Divide', *Seminar,* October 90, Issue No. 374, p. 25.

Shah, A.B., "The Facts of Communalism", *The Secularist,* No. 8, December 1970, p. 48.

Shahabuddin, Syed, "Rajiv and Ram Rajya", *Muslim India,* Vol. 105, September 1991, p. 29.

Shakir, Moin, "Communalism and Secularism in Indian Politics", *Teaching Politics,* Vol. 11, No. 12, 1985, pp. 3-23.

______, "On National Integration", *Social Scientist,* Vol. 10, No. 4, April 1982.

Sharma, B.K., "Communalisation of the Indian Police: Causes, Consequences and Remedies", *Political Science Review,* Vol. 27, No. 1-4, January-December, 1988.

Sharma, R.P., "Indira Gandhi and National Integration", *Journal of Social Science,* North-Eastern Hill University, Vol. 5, No. 3, July-September 1987, pp. 17-21.

Sharma, R.S., "Communalism and India's Past", *Social Scientist,* Vol.18, Nos. 1-2, January-February 1990, pp. 3-12.

Singh, Ajay, "Communalism and Party Politics", *Seminar* No. 388, December 1991, pp. 38-40.

Singh, Amar Kumar, "Communalism in India: A Socio-Psychological Analysis", *India International Centre Quarterly,* Vol. 7, No. 3, September 1980, pp. 157-164.

Singh, Gopal, "Socio-Economic Bases of Punjab Crisis", *Economic and Political Weekly,* Vol. 19, No. 1, January 7, 1984, p. 42.

Singh, Gusharpal, "Understanding the Punjab Problem", *Asian Survey,* Vol. 27, No. 12, December 1987, pp. 1268-1277.

Singh, Pritam, "Lessons of Panchayat at Elections", *Economic and Political Weekly,* Vol. 18, No. 43, October 22, 1983, pp. 1822-1823.

______, "Growing Separatist Trend", *Economic and Political Weekly,* Vol. 19, No. 5, February 4, 1984, pp. 195-196.

Singh Randhir, "Theorising Communalism: A Fragmentary Note in the Marxist Mode", *Economic and Political Weekly,* Vol. 23, No. 3, 23 July 1988.

______, "Communalism and the Struggle Against Communalism: A Marxist View", *Social Scientist,* Vol. 18, Nos. 8-9, August-September 1990.

Shourie, Arun, *The Indian Express*, November 12, 1989.

Srinivas, M.H., "On Living in a Revolution", *Economic and Political Weekly,* Vol. 26, No. 13, March 30, 1991.

______, "The Cohesive Role of Sanskritisation", *Contributions to Indian Sociology,* No. 1, 1957.

Srimanjari, "Seminar on Communalism in India: A Report", *Social Scientist,* Vol. 18, Nos. 6-7, June-July 1990, pp. 49-72.

Thapar, Romila, "Politics of Religious Communities", *Seminar* No. 365, January 1990, pp. 27-31.

______, "Communalism and the Historical Legacy: Some Facets", *Social Scientist,* Vol. 18, Nos. 6-7, June-July 1990.

______, "Religion, Culture and Nation", *Seminar* 377, January 1991, pp. 38-40.

______, "Historical Realities", *Seminar* 329, January 1987, pp. 45.

Tarkunde, V.M., "Hindu Communalism: Is it the Beginning of Fascism?" *The Times of India,* New Delhi, May 30, 1990.

Tyagi, Deshbandhu, "Gandhian Alternative of Communal Disharmony", *Political Science Review,* Vol. 28, Nos. 1-2, January-June 1989.

Vajpayee, Anil Kumar, "Emergence of the BJP: Confusion Regarding Causes", *Indian Journal of Political Science,* Vol. 51, No. 4, October-December 1990.

Verma, S.L., "Dimensions of Rising Communalism in India During the Eighties", *Political Science Review,* Vol. 25, Nos. 1-2, January-June 1986, pp. 9-31.

Weiner, Myron, "Congress Restored: Continuities and Discontinuities in Indian Politics", *Asian Survey,* Vol. 12, No. 4, April 1983, pp. 399-355.

Zaidi, Smia, "Caste and Politics in an Indian Village", *Social Change,* Vol. 20, No. 1, March 1990.

Pamphlets and Reports by NGOS

Chattopadhyay, Kunal, (ed.), *The Genocidal Programme in Gujarat: Anatomy of Indian Fascism,* Vadodara: Inquilabi Communist Sangathan, 2002.

Goyal, D.R., *Communalism v/s Nationalism: The Nehru Approach,* New Delhi: Sampradyaikta Virodhee Committee, 1970.

Gupta, Nand Lal, (ed.), *Nehru on Communalism,* Delhi: Sampardayikta Virodhee Committee, 1965.

Joshi, Subhadra, *Is RSS Behind Communal Riots? Saffron Conspirary,* Delhi: Sampradyikta Virodhee Committee.

______, *National Integration: The Communalist Way? Can We Allow It?,* Delhi: Sampradayikta Virodhee Committee, 1968.

Mathur, Girish, *Communal Violence: A Study in Political Perspective,* Delhi: Sampradayikta Virodhee Committee, 1968.

Noorani, A.G., *How Does a Riot Begin and Spread?,* New Delhi: Sampradayikta Virodhee Committee, 1970.

Rao, Ayde Shivaji, *Communal Riots in India: A Legal, Sociological and Political Study,* New Delhi: Sampradayikta Virodhee Committee.

'Who is Guilty'? Report of PUCL on 'Delhi Riots', November 1984.

'Bhagalpur Riots', Report of PUDR on Bhagalpur Riots 1989.

Report of PUCL on Delhi Riots, "Who are the guilty?", New Delhi, 1984.

PUDR Report, Bhagalpur Riots, Delhi, April 1990.

Pamphlet by Vishwa Hindu Parishad entitled "Chetanvani Desh Ko Khatra", New Delhi.

INDEX